LESTER PIGGOTT

JAMES LAWTON

ARTHUR BARKER LIMITED

A subsidiary of Weidenfeld (Publishers) Limited

Published in Great Britain by Arthur Barker Limited
91 Clapham High Street, London SW4 7TA

ISBN 0 213 16761 1

Printed in Great Britain by
Butler & Tanner Ltd
Frome and London

Contents

Acknowledgements

Trying to capture the career and life of Lester Piggott is a humbling experience and could not have been attempted without the tremendous help and encouragement of Ken Lawrence, Sports Editor of the *Daily Express*, who made available the newspaper's library Peter O'Sullevan, the racing writer and commentator who is closer to Piggott than any other journalist, gave vital help when it was most necessary. I am indebted to researcher Barry Cohen and the Misses Frances Jennings and Frances Russell, whose typing and spelling brought some coherence to the manuscript. John Morgan, former Sports Editor of the *Daily Express*, John Garnsey, Hilda Marshall and the *Express* racing staff were generous with their assistance.

The photographs in this book were reproduced by kind permission of the following (numbers refer to illustration pages):

Allsport (Tony Duffy): 12 *above*
Fox Photos: 1, 2 *above*, 4 *below right*, 5 *below*
Popperfoto: 2 *below*, 3, 4, 6, 7 *above*, 8 *below*, 9, 11 *above*
Sporting Pictures: 10, 11 *below*
Syndication International: 5 *above*, 7 *below*, 8 *above*, 12 *below*

Introduction

I knew early that Lester Piggott would be one of the world's great jockeys. One could not say precisely how great, you understand; whether he would quite have the courage and the cunning of Fred Archer, the dash and the flair of Steve Donoghue, the tireless fluency of Sir Gordon Richards. One could not guess how many times Piggott would win the Derby, how many times there would be a great communal catching of the breath on the downs and the muttered word that Piggott was coming, sleek bottom in the air, whip hand raised, wrists like iron.

I did not then know the trail of glory he would cut from Longchamp to Washington DC, but I knew about his greatness. I had it on the very best authority: my grandfather told me. I was six years old and my grandfather knew everything. He knew about the bare knuckle-fighters of his youth, Pedlar Palmer's gallantry and skill, the trenches of the Somme, what it was like to see Prussian lances glinting in the first morning sun – and there was a light in his eyes when he told me about this twelve-year-old boy who had just won his first race at Haydock Park, a few miles down the East Lancashire road.

My grandfather was a Warrington man. The town is part of the grey sprawl of South Lancashire. It makes steel wire and chemicals and it strips young men of illusions and fancy. Warrington was the home town of Steve Donoghue, and my grandfather knew about him too.

On this evening in August 1948 my grandfather came in from the races and announced; 'I've seen a boy today who could be as great as Steve Donoghue. His name is Lester Piggott. You should have seen him bring home his winner. You wouldn't credit he was just twelve years old. My, but he was determined.'

It happened in so many different ways, this implanting of the name Lester Piggott in millions of British households: a snatch of newsreel, word of mouth, a widening spread of newsprint, all matching the swell of achievement. Long ago Lester Piggott became more than a fine jockey, perhaps the finest who ever launched a horse into that last thrilling rush for the post.

J.L.
January 1980

1 Something in the Blood

Lester Piggott has entered the very spirit of the nation. Mood and fashion have changed many times since 1948 but there has always been Piggott. When he won his first race Clement Attlee was in Downing Street, India was violently shaking away from the British Empire, and Denis Compton was a dazzling, brilliantined young man. Piggott has never courted us, never sought our favours, never flattered us with his attention. He has never been winsome or trifled with false modesty. He has done it with a staying-power which is arguably unique in professional sport.

Only in his face, which once prompted comparison with a well-kept grave, is there a glimpse of the cost. The skin is of parchment. The smile, when it appears at all, is always enigmatic and usually wintry. His humour is tough, subtle, and bleak. About his nature there is an aloofness which was once expressed, chillingly, when he was fourteen years old. He said, 'I do not find my defective hearing a great handicap. You see, it has this advantage ... when I lose interest in what a person is saying I do not bother to read his lip movements.'

How can a nation continue to pour out mingled respect and affection, so apparently unrequited for more than thirty years? Piggott has been ruthless, contemptuous, and indifferent to the feelings of others. He has not been noticeably compassionate to the horses which provided a vehicle for his greatness. He once said, 'I regard horses as cunning creatures and they have got to be mastered. I treat a racehorse as a machine. To get the best service from a machine you treat it carefully. It is the same with racehorses. Father has taught me that if you make a pet of a racehorse it will go soft and silly and will not win races.'

His special hold on the public is in fact easily explained. Lester Piggott is highly esteemed because, in an age of dwindling achievement, of disappearing craft, he offers a rare and dazzling prospect. He offers the sight of a man relentlessly at work, declaring that here, at least, is something that will not wither through indifference or sagging pride. It has been suggested that there is a quite spectacular meanness about Piggott's nature; that he is motivated by nothing more elevated than a ceaseless need to accumulate money. It may be so. It may be true that valets have been kept waiting for their money, taxi-drivers have groaned at the miserly scale of his tips, that his idea of relaxation is a skim through the pages of the *Financial Times*. But all this is a matter between Piggott and his valets, his taxi-drivers, and his bank managers. People do not look for charm or charity in Lester Piggott; they look for a superb practitioner, a man about whom they can be sure in an age when certainties are rare.

The pride, the thrust, the absolute commitment to victory sent a small buzz around Haydock Park on the afternoon of 18 August 1948. Very quickly, the buzz changed to thunder, a storm of acclamation which gathered strength down the years and now, at the great meetings, can be overwhelming.

At Haydock Park the first surprise at the boy's feel, his maturity, and the strength of his finish on a mediocre three-year-old filly was diluted by the most cursory glance at his family history. For Donoghue, brought up in the huddled streets of a factory town, and Richards, of a mining stock, the turf was a wild dream, an escape from a life of grey to one of rainbow colours where the grass was fresh and crisp, the silks and the coats of the animals glowed and the women were soft-skinned and perfumed. For Piggott it was simply an inheritance, a right of destiny transmitted through generations.

He was by a Piggott out of a Rickaby, which is to say he was bred for everything: the classics, the jumps, the class and the courage the steel and the resilience. The male line ran back to the Day family of the late eighteenth century, trainers and jockeys touched with flair and a hint of villainy who merged with the legendary Cannons. Tom Cannon, a worthy adversary of the immortal Fred Archer, rode 1,544 winners. He won the Two Thousand Guineas four times, the Thousand Guineas three times, the Oaks four times, and the St Leger once. Travelling back through the lineage of Lester Piggott you have to linger with Tom Cannon for the most striking evidence of genetic power, which may slumber in one generation, then come vibrantly alive in another. You settle on Derby Day 1882, the supreme moment in the career of Lester Piggott's brilliant ancestor.

The downs throbbed. They formed a cloth of gold – and a hundred different shades. The old stand was packed tight, an open-topped sardine tin atop Regency pillars. Where the double-decker buses stand now, there were tents and flags. The flags proclaimed privilege. In the Tate Gallery there is a lovely work by W.P. Frith. He has all of it, the splendour and the squalor, the carriages, the fine dresses, the parasols, and the ragged shawls of the urchins looking wide-eyed at the toffs and their picnics of quails' eggs and smoked salmon and fine wine.

On Derby Day 1882 most eyes were fixed on Bruce, who had been idle as a three-year-old, but had shown much class in an unbeaten two-year-old career, beating Marguerite, who had gone on to carry the Thousand Guineas. As anticipated by his trainer, Bruce struck the front and ran powerfully down the hill. But he had a handicap which was to prove overwhelming. He had a jockey called Sammy Mordan. Tom Cannon was aboard Shotover in the colours of the Duke of Westminster. The filly had made an indifferent start to her career, but had improved dramatically, winning the Two Thousand Guineas, and going close in the Thousand Guineas. Cannon rode with a marvellously easy touch. He kept Shotover close up on Bruce. The racing historian Raymond Mortimer gives a lacerating account of Mordan: 'A curious, lisping little man who habitually referred to himself in the third person, Mordan was a very moderate jockey and on this occasion he rode even worse than usual.'

Some went so far as to suggest that the hapless Mordan was in league with a bookmaker; others ascribed his strange behaviour at Tattenham Corner to Bruce being distracted by a piece of paper blowing in the wind. Whatever the reason, Bruce took a tortuously wide route round Tattenham Corner. By contrast, Cannon had Shotover beautifully placed and over the last furlong he eased away from Quicklime to win by three-quarters of a length.

It was riding of the highest quality and it persuaded some critics that the margin between Cannon and the great Archer was narrow indeed. Cannon showed that day what it is to perfect the art of race riding, a sublime mix of nerve and timing and an implicit understanding of the capacity of a horse. The great trainer Noel Murless, a profound influence on the career of Lester Piggott, once said: 'You can teach a jockey many things, but there is something you cannot transmit. It is the feeling, the sensitivity of a natural jockey. It is a great mystery which only the horse, the great jockey, and God can really know about.'

On that Derby Day Piggott's forebear showed that there was no mystery for him. Lester Piggott, astonishingly, was to make the same point at Epsom eight times before even a hint that his career, the excellence of his judgement and the uncanny precision of his timing, was on the wane.

Cannon's three sons, Mornington, Kempton and Tom, were all successful jockeys. His daughter Margaret married Ernie Piggott, son of a Cheshire farmer, whose greatest pleasure was to ride, train, and deal in horses. The Piggotts set up their own dynasty. Of their sons, Ernest won the Grand National three times, Charles trained the 1939 Champion Hurdle winner, African Star, ridden at Cheltenham that day by Keith. Keith Piggott rode five hundred National Hunt winners and trained the Grand National winner Ayala. He was fearless and canny.

Keith Piggott's wife, Iris Rickaby, brought her own imposing blood line. For four generations in her family there had been trainers and jockeys. Her great-grandfather trained a Derby winner. Her grandfather won the Oaks. Her father, Fred Rickaby, was a famous jockey, and her nephew

Bill was to operate impressively, although somewhat below her son Lester, until his retirement in 1968. When Keith Piggott married Iris Rickaby at Hove on 16 September 1929 the bride's mother proudly told the gossip-columnists, 'This is a real racing romance. My daughter is a fine horsewoman. Twice she has won the Newmarket Town Plate.'

It was not really a marrying time. The world had come off its hinges; Wall Street was tumbling, America shivered and starved, and the wind from the west was biting. For most young people the Charleston might have belonged to another century. Suddenly, it was hard to be flippant. But there would always be racing; kids might be pinched and miserable but there would always be oats and training fees and riding presents. The Piggotts were bolstered by generations of prudence. When Lester's grandfather Ernest died in 1967, aged eighty-eight, he left £55,900.

Lester was born on 5 November 1935. He was a typical only child, serious-minded, and a tendency to content himself with his own company was reinforced by partial deafness and a resulting speech impediment. His parents took him to a specialist who concluded that the boy had a hearing age of a sixty-year-old man. Nature, in fact, was to prove a severe handicapper. He grew tall (for a jockey) and his face had a disconcerting roundness. Also, he had a sweet tooth. It was one of his few concessions to real childhood, and something to recall when considering the strength of mind and sheer determination which took him through so many years of murderous wasting. He was devoted to a pair of kittens, given to him by his mother, and the New Forest ponies, Brandy and Rip, on whose backs he first hinted of the future.

He was a remarkably neat child. On his bedside table there was a modern version of the Bible and, before they were supplanted by the *Racing Calendar* and form books, a perfectly folded pile of comics. He had a taste for Westerns, particularly those which featured the taming of mustangs. His dressing-table exuded organization. He didn't care for the cinema; television left him unmoved. He disliked the smell and the clatter of the town and loved the country, in an abstract way. He didn't go bird-nesting, didn't boast of a famous conker, didn't take to the woods with toy guns. He did eventually own an air-gun, which was polished and greased religiously.

When Lester was a few years old the family moved from Wantage to a big house in Lambourn, a few miles away on the Berkshire downs. Lester was distant from his schoolmates at King Alfred's, Wantage, which he attended before going to Miss Westlake's private school in Lambourn. The deafness and the faulty speech were the main causes of this, but there was something else. It was a kind of inner knowledge, as though he knew early what he wanted from life and there was no time, or need, to bother with certain trivialities. Sometimes his father would see the boy, quite alone, peering across the rolling downs. He was a lonely figure, but it wasn't a vulnerable, heart-rending loneliness calculated to upset the boy's parents. It was the aloofness of the true loner rather than that of the rejected or the inadequate.

When Lester was three years old his father put him on the back of the pony Brandy. It was a moment of sudden emotion in the life of Keith Piggott. Men who ride under National Hunt rules tend not to be emotional; the spills, the broken limbs, the bruising, and the brave horses who fall badly knock it out of a man. But there was a thickening in Keith Piggott's voice that day when he turned to his wife and said: 'Iris, it appears that we have bred a jockey.'

There may have been an element of wishful thinking as young Lester trotted the pony around the stableyard. But there was the instinct of Keith Piggott, too; the insight which comes with your blood and your life. Whatever it was, Keith Piggott, rider and trainer of racehorses, became also the trainer of a great jockey.

Lester's education was skimpy by most standards, but he learned enough. His hearing did not help the academic process, and he could not easily mix in childish games. But much of this seemed irrelevant. By the time he was twelve everybody knew it, not least the boy himself. Lester Piggott was going to be a jockey.

He learned the ways of a stable, rising as the first streaks of pink touched the dawn sky over the downs. There was the drudgery of course, the feeding, the cleaning of the boxes. There were chores of strictly limited appeal, like washing the hooves and genitals of the horses. But there was the sheer exhilaration of the working of the string and the liberating joy of a good, strong gallop, when all the boredom of routine shrivelled away. Above all, there was the absorbing, endless quest for knowledge of horses; he had to learn about their moods, their caprices. He had to get their measure so that he was able to dictate to them, rather than be carried along.

In front of him still was the moment when he was to put his burgeoning skill against the top men, Richards, Smirke, Breasley and Doug Smith. And not only the top men, of course; there were so many sub-layers of jockeyship, so many men who knew every inch of the British racecourses. It was one thing to ride in the haunting beauty of a Berkshire morning, to listen, straining that flawed hearing, for the rhythm of the hoofbeats. It would be something else to judge the pace, to gather the speed of a horse and then release it for the line at exactly the right moment.

Keith Piggott was encouraged by the shaping of Lester. He liked the coolness. He liked the single-mindedness. When he was six the boy tore away to victory in a children's race at a Red Cross charity event. His blue eyes shone in triumph. He would not swap this for a thousand Saturday matinees. He was the lion of the local gymkhanas.

By 7 April 1948 Keith Piggott had decided it was time to go; time to make the only meaningful measurement of the boy's progress. He put him on the back of The Chase at Salisbury. It was no spectacular début, but the boy performed capably. His nerve held and he rode The Chase at Bath, Kempton Park, and Worcester. On each occasion he deepened his knowledge of that particular animal and the peculiar pressures of race riding, and each time he edged closer to the frame. At Chepstow he rode Secret Code into second place. He came into the unsaddling enclosure of the pretty course in the Wye Valley, shyly acknowledging a word or two of congratulation. He resembled one of the choirboys he would have joined in Lambourn Church but for his deafness. It was the last time he would leave a racecourse other than as a sensation, a celebrity, or a source of fierce controversy.

The Chase was 10–1 for the Wigan Lane Selling Handicap at Haydock Park. Lester was alongside some formidable opposition. There was Billy Nevett, a scourge of the northern tracks, who at forty-three was a man strong in his own backyard and reluctant to yield to any southern challenge, especially when it was presented by a fair-haired twelve-year-old who blushed when he was addressed. There was too, the tough, vastly experienced Joe Sime.

Piggott rode flawlessly. Smoothly away at the start of the mile race he got to the pace of the thirteen-strong field and five furlongs out moved The Chase into top gear – and held her in a good rhythm. He won by a length and a half. There was a small crowd around the winner's enclosure and there was a ripple of cheers when he came in. He touched his cap. His cheeks were flushed. He said, 'It was terrific. I rode the last five furlongs hard and managed to pull ahead.'

He changed from his silks in the spartan jockey's room with its white plastered walls and a jumble of small-size clothes. He was 4 ft 6 ins tall and weighed 5 st 4 lb. He had put up 26 lb deadweight. He reran the race in his mind's eye, savouring that moment when he went clear and knew that he would hold it. There was the odd slap on his back, a muttered word of acknowledgement.

Racing is not a place where praise gushes. Tribute is a rivulet which only gathers force down the years. Its source had never before been the winning of a seller at Haydock Park but jockeys and trainers sensed something special about the Piggott kid. Even then he had an aura. Hugh McIlvanney later wrote in *The Observer*: 'He maintains a distance between himself and his admirers, but the impression of an intense privacy and, above all, of a fire burning under the iceberg, adds to the drama of his persona. He has the gunfighter's independence and authority, and much of his mystery.' In those early days it was seen as mere coltish diffidence, the insecurity of youth heightened by the sharp sense of isolation which comes with deafness. It wasn't long before it was possible to measure the scale of this lack of perception, but first there was a story tailored for the needs of the popular newspapers.

Since the war only Prince Charles, an out-and-out stayer with a somewhat captive audience, and Tommy Steele, a flashy five-furlong performer, have rivalled Piggott for early press exposure. Piggott's story was one of a boy wonder and for a heady moment there was a misapprehension that he was the youngest jockey ever to win. But his ancestor, Tom Cannon, had won at the age of nine.

Lester Piggott was some way from euphoria on the long drive home to Berkshire. He sat beside his father in the horse-box. For a time he read the *Sporting Life*. He glanced at a comic. Mostly he watched the country floating by, the flat Midlands, the factories and mile upon mile of alien brick and mortar. His spirit wilted at the thought of this way of life. But time and again that spirit was revived by the thoughts of the afternoon, the winning-post sliding into view and the weakening challenge from behind. By the time the horse-box was back in his native hills the boy was sleepy. He pecked at supper.

His mother told the *Daily Express*:

> He's just an ordinary boy. Don't make a fuss of him. He's done nothing special. He wants to be a jockey but he is in the middle of his schooldays and he will have to be back with his books at Miss Westlake's private school when the summer holiday is over. My husband trains about twenty horses and Lester spends most of his spare time in the stables. He gets up at seven and helps to exercise the horses before going to school. He has been riding since he was three and he is pretty good – though not a patch on his father.

The parental mood was maintained by Keith Piggott, who said, 'He won't be able to take up racing seriously until he is fifteen. There is no reason why he should not be a good jockey.'

The boy was in bed by 10.30 pm. His bedroom was as well

ordered as ever. He folded his clothes meticulously. He went straight to sleep. Downstairs his parents speculated how long they could maintain the fiction that their son was just an ordinary boy.

2 Sweet Taste of Zucchero

Zucchero never had Nijinsky's class, Sir Ivor's turn of foot, and you couldn't begin to compare his heart with that of Roberto. You will not find Zucchero in any list of great horses. You will not even find him in any list of Lester Piggott's great horses – except perhaps in one written out by the man himself. The fact is that Zucchero was to the shaping of Lester Piggott what the first battle is to a trained fighting man. After it he knows he is so much stronger. He knows what he can do. He has proved something to himself.

Zucchero was the sort of colt which leaves a trainer suspended between heaven and hell. He was bay, stood sixteen hands, and moved beautifully – when in the mood. His trainer Bill Payne recalls, 'When he was happy with himself, and his rider, he was lovely to see. He just stroked the ground.' The trouble was that Zucchero's moods were as fitful as the sun which plays across the White Horse Hill gallops at Lambourn. When the sun is out White Horse Hill is a glory of nature. When the sun moves behind the clouds, the hill looks sombre, full of foreboding.

'Zucky' explored the outer reaches of eccentricity on White Horse Hill. He hated to be forced. If you tried it you learned a new dimension to the word cussed. Use a whip on him and you could do not better than say a brief prayer. Physically, he was not a stunner. Payne says, 'His forelegs were not the prettiest. They were a bit straight and he turned them out a bit. But his action was so wonderfully smooth he never hurt himself. The problem was that he needed more understanding than any horse I have ever known.'

Trainer Ken Cundell parted with him at the end of his three-year-old career. He did so with great misgivings. He knew that there was gold buried down there in the emotional chaos. The colt had talent which could make your blood pulse, bring you in from the gallops with dreams of glory. But a trainer has to measure his time, consider the potential of each of his string. It is rather similar to the role of the coach of a football team who has to compare the virtues of the star who has a tendency to empty a bottle of vodka on match morning with those of the honest performer who might just find something extra. The trainer has, of course, additional complications, not least the fact that each owner believes that his particular horse is destined to stride out into the Elysian fields of racing history. In the event there was some disagreement between Cundell and owner George Rolls. Cundell didn't need telling that Zucchero had something. But there is a limit to the time you can spend with a horse who isn't even certain to leave the start. There had been a crushing disappointment in the 1951 Derby when Zucchero, a 28–1 shot, appeared disdainful of the whole, noisy affair. He was left hopelessly at the start.

Zucchero left Cundell and moved to Payne's Seven Barrows yard in Lambourn. When Bill Payne took over Zucchero he knew he had one chance. It was for a rider to reach down into the nature of the horse and make real contact. It would be an extraordinary achievement, one which, for example, had proved beyond the scope of the vastly experienced and not noticeably under-confident Charlie Smirke.

Payne had a hunch that there was someone who might do it. Young Lester Piggott might do it. Payne had been best man at the wedding of Keith and Iris Piggott. He had watched the boy grow up and followed his infant career with a sharp interest. He had been one of the trainers eager to use this precocious apprentice who so quickly emerged as one of the key riders in England. He had detected a special talent in the boy. It was that quality which Sir Noel Murless says is the preserve of the great jockeys – the subliminal knowledge of a horse, the capacity to understand completely its personality and its instincts. Payne was sure he had seen this in Piggott. Though it was true that the fifteen-year-old Lester had been aboard Zucchero at the Derby fiasco, Payne reckoned that his intuition would carry him through the job. He gambled that Piggott could do the reaching down to make vital contact with Zucchero.

The cussed Zucchero and the aloof young Lester made the contact all right. The beast became a beauty. He was second in the King George VI and Queen Elizabeth Stakes at Ascot, which was then Britain's most valuable race. He won the Rose of York Stakes twice, the Princess of Wales Stakes, and the Coronation Cup in 1953, beating the much fancied French contender Dynamite.

In the Coronation Cup Zucchero reversed the outcome of the first running of the Washington International at Laurel Park, when he was beaten by Wilwyn. At Epsom Wilwyn was a well beaten third. At the pinnacle of his career Piggott was to perform rides of sheer brilliance at Laurel, but he might have scored sensationally there on Zucchero in 1952 had Ken Cundell not enforced his retaining rights and asked the boy to ride at Sandown Park. The point is a mere historical footnote, like saying that the Army secretary kept Wellington out of a useful skirmish on the road to Waterloo. But the significance of Zucchero was immense. He was the first man-size challenge in the career of Lester Piggott and the challenge was met with a delicacy of touch which spoke dramatically of greatness.

Payne will never forget the memory of Piggott and Zucchero picking off the field of the Coronation Cup.

It was a superb ride. You can only really grasp how superb it was when you know all the difficulties presented by Zucchero. If a jockey was at all fidgety, showed any impatience, well, that was the end of it as far as old Zucky was concerned.

In his own way Lester got to love the horse. He was so patient. Of course his timing has become a legend. In those days his whole technique was coming together, taking shape, and it was wonderful to watch the process. I was at the start of the Coronation Cup – the danger area for us. I was delighted by the start. Zucchero was off smoothly.

When I got to the other side of the course, I went straight to the jockey's room. You could go through then. Lester was sitting there on his own. He didn't say much in those days – he doesn't say that much now. But this day he had one of the biggest smiles I've ever seen on his face. He just said, 'Well, we showed 'em, then.'

For those who knew the rhythms of racing, it was the true point of arrival. At seventeen the boy had proved that the years of promise were not illusory; they were the foundation of something which reached beyond Iris Piggott's concept of an 'ordinary boy'.

Victory on The Chase at Haydock Park had been the one win in 1948. But in twenty-four outings he had not displeased his father or any of the trainers who had called on his services. It was noted how calm he was, how quickly he absorbed instructions and how faithfully he carried them out. Quite soon the need to pass on precise riding instructions to Lester Piggott would become unnecessary to all but the foggiest of trainers. In the meantime it was a fine quality, this ability to translate perfectly the advice of the man who had prepared the horse for action. By 1949 the boy was besieged by riding offers. As a schoolboy he had problems of availability, but he did manage to accept 120 rides, winning six, finishing second eight times, and third on thirty-nine occasions. The ratio of wins was less than miraculous, but all the work was accomplished vigorously and not one trainer was able to claim, even after the reassurance of a whisky or two, that his horse might have won with someone more experienced aboard.

By 1950 – when the school leaving age was fourteen years old – he was clear of the restrictions of the classroom and his celebration of freedom was spectacular. He sailed through to the Apprentice Championship, winning fifty-two races and utterly dwarfing his rivals. His winning haul came from four hundred rides. The statistics are impressive enough but they do not reveal the fierce, thrilling style which even caught the imagination of those who considered racing no more than a passing distraction. It was such an intriguing style, so finely balanced between sublety and a kind of savage intensity, there was no need to know the intricacies of racing to grasp how thoroughly it was impregnated with the urge to win.

Some feared that the boy would burn himself out or injure himself badly. There was much evidence to support these fears. He began to collect suspensions ... and injuries. He cracked his collar-bone at Lincoln at the start of the 1951 season, came back at a speed which staggered some tough veterans, and his season ended early at Lingfield in August when his horse fell and he broke his collar-bone again – and a leg. People thought Piggott was too ambitious, that his determination to win was blinding him to all the normal restraints and cautions of the game. This made Keith Piggott simmer. He could only see a boy filled with the optimism and the courage of youth.

His boy couldn't understand why it was wrong to go for a narrow gap in the field. If he saw daylight he went for it. It all seemed so simple, so elementary to him. Was racing a matter of 'after you, Charles' or a fiercely competitive way of life in which men could be made or ruined in the course of one afternoon?

He sensed that some of his more experienced, and less gifted, rivals resented his sudden impact, his swift progress to acclaim. Every morning the popular newspapers carried some new snippet from the life of Master Piggott, a coverage unparalleled until that of tennis prodigy Tracey Austin some thirty years later. 'It's not my fault I'm a kid who can play with the big stars,' she said at one point. 'Some of them can be so bitchy. They talk about my dresses and my pigtails. It can be pretty cruel.' Piggott was also a kid who could play with the big stars. The difference was that Piggott simply kept playing – as long as his elders considered he wasn't playing too roughly. Had Piggott made an outburst it would certainly have been directed at the stewards, who seemed alarmed by the rapidity of the boy's fame. Although from time to time some of the jockeys felt the need to object to some of young Piggott's more excessive optimism, the jockeys' room consensus was that the kid was committing no greater crime than impatience. Few doubted that his reputation would grow surely, that his fiery nature would ultimately be cooled by the extraordinary level of his talent.

But if Piggott's impact in the jockeys' room was unusually powerful for one so young, his effect in the factories and the pubs could only be described as phenomenal. Fleet Street bombarded the public with snippets about the 'boy wonder'. Within racing there was horror at the instant glory; one of racing's leading historians, Roger Mortimer, grumpily announced that the attention the boy was receiving was 'nauseating'. It was a matter of opinion, of course, and the British public showed no such reservations. They eagerly followed the boy's progress from his first victory through such milestones as his leaving school and fifteenth birthday party. The picture which emerged struck many as unnaturally bleak. Lester Piggott appeared to be a boy shorn of all the natural joys of youth. His fifteenth birthday party was without guests.

Mrs Piggott explained, 'We wanted him to have a party. But Lester lives in his world and only seems to come alive at race-meetings.'

'He gets four hours' riding every day, exercising the horses in my stables,' Keith Piggott said. 'That's quite enough for him. Three hours a day of lessons are quite sufficient for a coming jockey. At sixteen he will finish altogether with education. From then on it will all be racing.'

It was implied that the boy was being driven into a world of sacrifice and self-denial, but his parents saw that there could be no other way of life for their son. He didn't want guests at his birthday party. He was happy to go into the garden, prepare his bonfire and light his fireworks he had bought with his five shillings pocket-money on his own.

It was a high price, some claimed, for youthful fame, but concern was lost on the silent boy. He was friendless but he didn't pine for friendship. He appeared not to need such relationships. His parents knew this but the public saw only a schoolboy who was announcing an astonishingly mature talent, and they were fascinated. In a society weakened and wearied by years of war and rationing, made cynical by the promises of politicians, it should not have been so surprising that the young Piggott stood out as a symbol of optimism, an encouragement to a jaded generation. Nonetheless, many of the newspaper articles about the 'boy wonder' had overtones of outrage at the Piggotts' upbringing of Lester.

Throughout his career Piggott has always been angered by speculation about his nature and the way he lives. For him it has always been a case of one great imperative: he wants to ride, to be master of his destiny. What he did with his spare time was surely a matter for himself to decide.

I was riding at my father's place in Upper Lambourn as soon as I could walk. Everything always took second place to my education as a jockey. When I was at the village school I would ride work with the first lot, do my two horses, cycle three miles to school, and do the horses again when I got home. I love riding and the thrill of it all. This business of competing several times a day, of winning, has always been part of me.

I have often read that I am so good and dedicated because I have to make up for my deafness. That's a load of tripe in my book. People who do things well and become famous are always said to do so to compensate for something like an unhappy childhood, for their mother being shot or something.

The reason that I am where I am is that I work really hard and have exactly the right temperament. I have always been happy on my own.

A more pertinent issue was raised by John Rickman in the *Daily Mail* of 4 August 1951. Rickman suggested, with strong supporting evidence, that Piggott's physical development might prevent him from becoming England's champion jockey, a direction in which his talent seemed to be pointing him unequivocally.

Will the fifteen-year-old wonder boy jockey be the champion before he is twenty-one? This is the question that the racing world has been asking since this gifted lad made it plain last year that he was a starlet of the saddle. If he continues to grow and put on weight as he has done in the last three years, the answer must be: 'Possible but improbable'. One has only to look at photographs taken down the past years to see how Lester has shot up. He is now nearly the same height as Harry Wragg who was one of the tallest jockeys when he retired at the end of 1946, when his riding weight was in the neighbourhood of 8 st 7 lb.

At the time Rickman wrote this article, and voiced the general suspicion, Piggott was 5 ft and weighed 6 st 9 lb. Assuming normal weight gain, a weight of nine stone plus could be projected for his twenty-first birthday. He was later to become known as 'the Long Fella' because of his height.

But Rickman did not know the strength of Piggott's will. Piggott wouldn't, in fact, be champion jockey by his twenty-first birthday, but there would be a stage of his career when he would simply annex the title. He did it with thimbles of water, shavings of chicken breast, and a developing taste for sips of fine champagne and the best of Cuba's cigar industry. Piggott has wasted like few other men. The round face of boyhood would change quickly to the lined parchment. He would go to the sauna as a Trappist monk goes to his cell. He would fantasize over plump game, cuts of prime beef, and delicate desserts. And each day he would lose weight.

By the time Rickman came to write his piece Piggott's career was already laced with extraordinary deeds. His twenty-fifth winner, which came at Folkestone and moved him up the rungs to the status of 3 lb claimer, had left Sir Gordon Richards trailing home third. On 20 September 1950, the fourteen-year-old had become a fully-fledged jockey. There is no elaborate ceremony, nothing, for example, like the ritual which accompanies the novillero's transition to full matador. But Piggott didn't need ritual or pomp. They could be assigned along with the birthday parties and frolics which sentimental columnists had mourned on his behalf.

His success in Brighton's Autumn Cup on Zina – which marked the end of his apprentice allowances – brought a more familiar crowd around the winners' enclosure than the one which had greeted him at Haydock Park. He had lip-read the phrase 'Well done, Lester' many times now, but he was still touched and gave the small shy smile.

By the end of 1953 he had ridden 230 winners. He had co-existed brilliantly with Zucchero. In 1950 he had guided

Holmbush to victory in the Jockey Club Stakes, which was worth £5,400, then a considerable amount. In 1951 he had opened his empire-building days at Epsom with a win on Barnacle in the Great Metropolitan and at Sandown Park he had carried the Eclipse Stakes on Mystery IX.

He had ridden with a marvellous panache to take Zina within a neck of winning the 1950 Cambridgeshire. Had he done so it would have been an act of sheer flamboyant defiance, for he rode under the shadow of a suspension which would leave him grounded for the rest of the season. Piggott was sure he had the verdict over Doug Smith, who was on Kelling. The boy wonder nosed Zina towards the winners' place in the Newmarket enclosure and when the news of the photo finish was announced his face showed a flash of disappointment, his upper lip a flicker of emotion. It was one of his last displays of youthful vulnerability.

Two years later there was not a glimpse of emotional frailty when he finished second in the 1952 Derby. Charlie Smirke was aboard the Aga Khan's fifth winner, Tulyar. Piggott lost it by three-quarters of a length. His blue eyes blazed at the end. He believed Tulyar had leaned into his mount, Gay Time. He wanted to object. The owner, Mrs J. V. Rank, and the trainer, Noel Cannon, had to cool him. There was no chance of the objection being upheld, he was told. He had ridden a fine race, said Cannon. Piggott should measure his progress in the game and be content with it. To be second in the Derby at sixteen was not exactly failure, but Piggott brooded heavily on the prize which had been claimed by his ancestors. And then he weighed in. He had been unseated as he passed the Derby finishing-post, and it took police and stable-lads twenty minutes to get Gay Time to the unsaddling enclosure. There was no light conversation on the drive back to Berkshire.

Piggott had an interesting winter after the Gay Time experience, which had been heavy with anti-climax. Smirke brought in Tulyar just ahead of him again in the King George VI and Queen Elizabeth Stakes. Piggott, obeying another dictate of his blood, took to hurdling. He won at Wincanton on Boxing Day and then in March 1954 he claimed one of the big prizes. He rode Prince Charlemagne, his Derby partner of 1953, to success in the Triumph Hurdle at Hurst Park.

It was another example of the range of Piggott's horsemanship and prompted some to speculate that his career might bear some resemblance to that of the fine jockey, Martin Molony, who was equally adept on the flat and over the jumps. The speculation was short lived. Keith Piggott knew the hazards of the jumps. He also knew the potential of his son in that area of racing where kings and millionaires clustered most thickly.

Zucchero, Gay Time, and Zina had been taken as far as they could go; Lester Piggott had shown that his destiny lay in the pursuit of great prizes. There was to be no tempting of fate over the timber. The promise of gold was so strong that only a fool would take unnecessary chances. You could call a Piggott mean, arrogant, ruthless, but never a fool.

3 Talk of the Devil

Talking to Lester Piggott gives you no inkling of the romance and the mystery of his work. He strips away so many of the colourful layers which mean so much to those who find themselves drawn to the turf. Riding winners is good, profitable work, he suggests, not some mystical tryst with destiny. But it is. Piggott deceives when he scowls and grunts at suggestions that his work, and his achievements, mean anything more to him than the most feasible way of earning a rich living.

As a boy he was asked: 'Which is your favourite racecourse?'

'Newbury,' came the reply, after a long, meditative pause.

'Is this', pressed the interviewer, 'because of the setting, the ground, the gentle roll of the course?'

'No,' said Piggott, 'it's nearest home.'

The deception is that Piggott never thinks beyond the detail of his job and the imperative need to win. The truth is that he has a powerful sense of history. When he came second in the 1952 Derby part of his frustration was that he had already, in his mind's eye, joined his illustrious ancestors, the Cannons, in the winning enclosure. There is a silver statuette of Fred Archer on a sideboard in Piggott's Newmarket home. It has the honoured place of a highly significant item. It reflects Piggott's admiration for the man who even now, ninety-four years after his tragic death, challenges the title of the greatest jockey the world has ever seen. We can be sure that Piggott knew, even in those days when he was first announcing his challenge to the great men, the scale of his task. He reveres the memory of Archer, salutes the deeds of another touched with tragedy, Steve Donoghue, and carries great respect for the man who dominated English jockeyship for thirty years, Sir Gordon Richards. But it is just as clear that Lester Piggott is aware of the ground he himself has covered, the extent to which he has obscured the work of his predecessors.

The three great challengers to Piggott's all-time supremacy, Archer, Donoghue and Richards, have already been mentioned. There have been many extraordinary horsemen in the history of the English turf, but Archer, Donoghue and Richards were the great historical triumvirate when the young Piggott came clattering into sight in the early fifties. They were the demigods of a profession which was without the trappings of celebrity in the seventeenth and eighteenth centuries, when a jockey was no more than a country lad who could be guaranteed to keep his seat, follow instructions, ask no questions, and tell no lies.

The country lad was cheap and willing and quite expendable. It was a talented if somewhat disreputable character called Sam Chifney who first established the influential role of the jockey and by 1836 the great Jem Robinson had won his sixth Derby – and proved that a jockey could be a man of vital skill and integrity. Chifney had a fine talent, too, but his vague grasp of morality led to much controversy and despite the backing of the Prince of Wales in one scrape, this marauding son of Norfolk ended his days in a debtors' prison.

Though Jem Robinson ushered in a new generation of jockeys, men of judgment whose feelings and instincts were accorded great respect by many trainers, there were many scandalous relapses in the trade. The famous Charles Wood fell in 1877, pulling down with him an ex-Jockey Club Steward. 'Gentlemen' riders were also known to let the side down. Roger Longrigg, in his work *The Turf*, says of one of them, George Baird alias Mr Abington, 'he liked bullies and trollops, in whose company he died prematurely and squalidly'. But it was true that the great jockey had arrived. Tom Cannon and his sons were to develop the concept. Fred Archer was to gloriously enshrine it. Few men of the past can have lived so vividly in the imagination of later generations.

Fred Archer was much more than a sportsman; he was one of the glories of his age. His talent carried him far beyond the narrow confines of his sport. So magical was this talent that even royalty was moved to something approaching reverence in his presence.

Archer's father was a Cheltenham innkeeper who had been a bold and successful steeplechase jockey, winning the Grand National of 1858. There are similarities between Archer and Piggott. Archer was tall (5 ft 10 ins) and had a personality which could move from introversion to a black-dog depression. By the age of twelve he had ridden his first winner. He, too, faced a career of wasting. His figure tended to balloon in the winter and every spring he had to remove as much as three stone. Such wasting would have ravaged the spirit of any man. Archer's achievement was to push back the day when it would become unbearably depressing. But before that day there was to be glory, so powerful it transcended the final hours of tragedy, living so strongly that to many devotees of racing today it is still a tangible force.

There was glory at Doncaster and the great climax of the English season, the St Leger. Six times he was roared home on the Town Moor, lifted up on shoulders, and then toasted to the small hours. He negotiated Epsom beautifully, always urgently away at the start, always smooth and handy at Tattenham Corner. He won the Derby five times, the Oaks four times. On Newmarket's Rowley Mile he was dominant, too, sweeping in with four Two Thousand Guineas and two Thousand Guineas winners. In only seventeen years he brought in 2,471 winners in 8,084 rides. The figures are stunning. But they give only a vague insight to the impact of Fred Archer. It was not that he was so stylish in the saddle, favouring a somewhat hunched forward method; the reason why he was fêted, why crowds gathered to cheer him on the way to the course, was that in his spirit and his bearing he proclaimed himself a winner.

He rode a finish which brought the hairs standing up on the backs of thousands of necks. He thought out a race in every detail. He could delay his killing effort to the last strides. There was a ruthless streak, too, and had his day been as sentimental as Piggott's he would surely have felt at one stage or another the hot breath of the RSPCA.

Society ladies would have gladly given a year's clothing and millinery allowance to have lifted him on to their hacks and cantered off to the woods. They were drawn to his brooding, somewhat sensual face, his air of detachment and the inevitable hint of mysterious, latent passion. He dressed soberly, in tweedy suits, and his hair was neatly parted, slightly left of centre. He was also the target of the legions of crooks who plagued the racecourses, wheedling, fixing, attempting to corrupt. They were given as little encouragement as the society ladies. Fred Archer was always his own man. As Lester Piggott was to do, Archer married the daughter of a trainer, John Dawson, whose brother Matt was the bridegroom's 'governor' and confidant for the rest of his short life. There was something untouchable about Fred Archer. No one could have been more immersed in the business, more anxious to steal a march at the start, to hinder a feared rival, than Fred Archer – yet in an unfathomable way he was above it all.

In 1885 his professional life reached a degree of perfection which has come to few sportsmen. He scored an astonishing 246 winners – a figure which was unbeaten until Gordon Richards pushed on to 259 in 1933; for his relentless performance he was given Archer's whip and spurs. But they couldn't quite sprinkle him with the same quality of stardust. Archer won his fourth Derby and three other classics in 1885. His guiding of Melton past the Epsom finishing-post is still considered one of the great Derby masterpieces.

Archer measured the triumph of Melton down to a head. It was a piece of uncanny judgment and its origin lay in the fact that Archer had ridden Melton's chief rival, Paradox, to a somewhat fortuitous win in the Two Thousand Guineas.

Archer established clearly in his own mind that not to cover Paradox, or keep him from the lead, until the last possible moment was the short route to disaster. The colt would lose interest and when the challenge came, as it inevitably would, rhythm would be lost beyond recall.

Archer's father-in-law trained Melton and the jockey felt no reluctance in switching from Paradox for the Derby. It was one of those glorious Derby days when the sky over the downs is a vast seamless blue. The roads to Epsom heaved, and choked, and ground to a standstill. Once again the nation expected something of Fred Archer. The betting men poured on the money. Melton was 75–40 favourite. Paradox, partnered by Fred Webb, a habitually unlucky rider who had been placed in the four previous Derbies, was 6–1. At Tattenham Corner the order was Xaintrailles, Red Ruin, Paradox, Luminary, Royal Hampton and Melton, whose rider had never let Paradox stray from his sights. Three furlongs out Fred Webb made his move. He sent Paradox to the front and immediately there was a surge of hope as the colt quickened nicely along the rails. Archer now had to make his last calculation. Imagine the fineness of this calculation and the difficulty of making it as you gallop through an ocean of faces, a thunder of noise. A furlong out Archer moved Melton to challenge. Paradox, true to form, had begun to waver but as Melton came alongside there was a flicker of new interest. He seemed to be holding Melton. Fred Webb, at last, was striding up the centre of the aisle. Archer wouldn't accept it. He lashed Melton. He got home by a head.

He went on to win the St Leger and at Epsom the following June he was aboard Ormonde, the Duke of Westminster's famous colt. Ormonde came to be a celebrity after his Derby success, which was by a length and a half over The Bard, ridden by Charles Wood. By the end of his racing career, in 1887, Ormonde was so famous it seemed reasonable that he should be guest of honour at a party thrown by the Duke of Westminster at his London home. The other guests included royalty and aristocracy from all over Europe and the East. Indian princes were said to have fed geraniums to Ormonde as he strode majestically through the gardens. The

Queen of the Belgians offered him a carnation, which he also found to his taste. It was a happy affair, at least for those who had recovered from the shock which had come the previous year: Fred Archer's death.

For many in England it was as though a light had been suddenly snapped off. The effects of wasting, plus a bout of typhoid fever, had brought him to the point of physical breakdown; mentally, he had never recovered from the death of his young wife in childbirth. He was feverish and slipped into moods of unbreakable depression. He stared out of the window of his sickroom but he could find no uplift, no hope, out there in the rolling country where he had once galloped with such a light heart. He could see only despair. He reached out for a revolver he had hidden in the room. His sister, who had been nursing him with ever-rising apprehension, screamed and fought him. He was terribly weak but he found, deep inside himself, the strength which had carried him to so many pulsating finishes on the racecourse. He drew the revolver from the desperate reach of his sister, placed it against his temple and fired. He was twenty-nine.

There was a vast scale to Fred Archer. He was more than anyone determined that a jockey should be more than a hireling, a little man to pat on the head and say 'well done, lad'. He prepared the ground superbly for Steve Donoghue, Sir Gordon Richards, and Lester Piggott.

Steve Donoghue, more spectacularly than any of Archer's successors, gloried in the new horizons. Born in the backstreets of Warrington in 1884, his youth was bleak and troubled. Donoghue's first glimpse of escape came when he tramped across the Cheshire fields and presented himself to the famous trainer John Porter, who was attending Chester races. His career as a stable-lad and precocious lightweight jockey was mixed.

He was erratic and somewhat hostile to discipline, but for every time one of his trainers had reason to lecture him there were three occasions when admiration for his riding technique, and his understanding of horses, was more appropriate. He emerged as a rider of power and tremendous panache. 'Come on, Steve' was a cry which became one of the catch phrases of the twenties and thirties. The foundation of his fame, his place in the great triumvirate, was laid by the astonishing hold he exerted on the Derby between 1921 and 1925, when he won four times on Humorist, Captain Cuttle, Papyrus, and Manna.

By 1921 Donoghue's services were fought over and he rode Humorist for Wantage trainer Charles Morton only after some skilful negotiating with Lord Derby, who had him on a retainer. The idea that a jockey, the son of a working man, might talk Lord Derby out of his rights would have been unthinkable at the dawn of Fred Archer's days. But Donoghue, like Archer, had a way with toffs. He counted them among his personal friends. His particular friends included Eleanor Lady Torrington, a striking ex-actress, and Jimmy White, the financier and theatrical impresario whose origins were also to be found in a poor Lancashire family. When Donoghue's reckless, always generous life-style led him to financial disaster Sir Victor Sassoon was willing to pick up the pieces.

In the 1921 Derby Donoghue rode Humorist to victory by a neck. It was a piece of riding which contained all the classic ingredients: timing, nerve, and power. But in this case there was another factor. Humorist, who so gamely mastered the challenge of Craig An Eran, was a dying horse. He was suffering from tuberculosis and only two weeks after his great day he had a haemorrhage of the lungs and died.

Another of Donoghue's successes in this extraordinary blaze of Epsom glory (later commemorated by the Steve Donoghue Gate to the main grandstand) revealed his absolute calm at critical moments. Captain Cuttle, a high-spirited colt, had shown signs of lameness going to the start, after Donoghue had dismounted in the paddock to discover that his mount had a broken plate. A blacksmith was called to perform emergency repairs. Donoghue's temperament remained unruffled during this last-minute crisis, and took Captain Cuttle to finish in 2 mins 34.6 secs – a new Derby record. Donoghue simply scooped up the race. He made the lead at Tattenham Corner and moved smoothly into the rising ground, beating Tamar by four lengths.

In 1923 Donoghue brought in Papyrus from Pharos by a length. It was one of the great battles along the Epsom straight. Donoghue had taken it up at Tattenham Corner, as he had the previous year with Captain Cuttle, but this time he had to reckon with a formidable challenge from Pharos. At two furlongs out he had a real problem on his hands. But his nerve and ability to coax out a final thrust were again flawless. He pulled away in the last strides to the post.

Donoghue and Papyrus later travelled to New York for a challenge race against the American champion Zev at Belmont Park. The American combination exploited home advantage and Papyrus was easily defeated on a muddy track. However, Papyrus was one of Donoghue's great horses, a point made eloquently enough when Parth, third behind Papyrus at Epsom, snapped up the not inconsiderable bauble of the Prix de l'Arc de Triomphe that autumn.

Donoghue won the 1925 Derby on Manna by eight lengths. It was his most comfortable triumph, not only in the matter of the winning margin but in the fact that Donoghue was able to gently turn on the pressure all the way from Tattenham Corner. As a two-year-old, Manna had been wilful and sometimes actively mischievous to the point of actually kicking the great trainer, Fred Darling. The gallops shook and rumbled when that news went abroad. Manna behaved impeccably from the first moment Steve Donoghue sat on his back.

However, Donoghue too was touched with tragedy. He had apparently endless charm and he loved the fine things that success could buy, but his marriage ended unhappily and before he died in 1945 he was racked by financial worries. He was the classic example of a sportsman whose zest for living, triggered by the exhilaration of those days at Epsom, would always prompt him to rediscover the thrill of such moments. Steve Donoghue must have been consoled by the knowledge that few men had travelled it with such verve and grace.

You could not use such words about Sir Gordon Richards. A Staffordshire man, one of eight children, his first riding came on ponies which his father bought for a pony-and-trap taxi service for the local station. At fifteen he went to Martin Hartigan's stables at Foxhill, Wiltshire. Hartigan was private trainer for Steve Donoghue's friend Jimmy White and Donoghue was allowed to ride the best of the crop. Donoghue was impressed by the Staffordshire lad, who was so keen, so correct, and gave Richards much encouragement. It was a crucial contribution to a career which was to dismantle so many records and was to be shaped by such legendary trainers as Fred Darling and Sir Noel Murless.

Free of wasting problems, Richards was champion jockey twenty-six times. He won 4,870 races out of 21,834. When Richards won his first Derby in 1953 on Sir Victor Sassoon's Pinza, beating the Queen's Aureole by four lengths, he was invited up to the royal presence. He had a glass of champagne, chatted with the new Queen and Prince Philip.

The previous month he had heard from Downing Street that he would be knighted. He had completed the journey first embarked upon by Fred Archer and the Cannons, carrying the art of jockeyship to a level of prestige which could not have been contemplated in the days of the roguish Chifney.

Just as Steve Donoghue had spotted his own potential so many years before, Richards had been taken with young Lester Piggott in the early fifties. He was astonished at the force of the boy, the extraordinary commitment. Now, a good career as a trainer and racing manager behind him, Richards could scarcely be more generous about the boy who thundered at his heels. It was one of history's more poetic touches that Piggott should win his first Derby in 1954, the year of Richards' retirement. It was as though the baton, or rather the whip, had been passed on. Sir Gordon well remembers the dazzling impression the young Piggott made on him.

> Even in those first days you could tell that Lester Piggott had a touch of the devil – and a touch of genius. What was so wonderful about him was his absolute determination. Of course he ran into trouble with stewards. It was inevitable, I suppose. If he saw a gap he would go through. If he didn't see a gap, and he couldn't

go inside, outside, over or under, he would just try to go through. He didn't seem to understand the notion of being a loser.

I admired the boy's attitude and what has happened since; the way his career has gone hasn't really surprised me. He had something no one could teach him. He was a natural with horses and he rode these wonderful finishes. I didn't see any cruelty. I just saw someone who understood horses very deeply and who knew how far he could take a particular horse.

Great jockeys, experienced trainers and the richest owners were all moved by his fiery assault on the game. He so impressed a bell-boy in the Waldorf Hotel in London that the latter complete changed his life. He too had to ride like Lester Piggott. I spoke to that boy in the late summer of 1979. He had put away his whip and boots for the last time. We spoke on the sweeping lawns of Thirty Acre Barn, the fine stables which are just a brief canter from Epsom Downs. The former bell-boy, owner of the stables, was looking forward to a new career as a trainer.

I suppose I owe everything to Lester Piggott. He was the inspiration, the magnet. If it hadn't been for him I wouldn't have ridden Mill Reef. I wouldn't have known what it's like in Calcutta and Bombay and Hong Kong and Australia. He did it for a whole generation of jockeys, you know, He gave us our ambitions and our hopes. He showed us what could be done. He was so brilliant, so exciting.

The former bell-boy is, of course, Geoff Lewis, one of the few modern jockeys whose name doesn't shrivel at the mention of Lester Piggott.

4 Never Say Die

There wasn't much time left for Joe Lawson as he surveyed the Newmarket gallops through the half-moon spectacles normally favoured by bank managers and headmasters. Nor for Robert Sterling Clark, sitting in a wheelchair in a nursing home surrounded by the skyscrapers of Manhattan. Lawson, trainer of racehorses, and Clark, industrialist and sportsman, were both in their seventies. They had achieved almost every target they had set for themselves in life – except the English Derby.

In the early summer of 1954 only Lester Piggott, aged eighteen, could afford to be totally objective about the Derby chances of Never Say Die, a powerfully built, American-bred chestnut colt of mediocre performance. 'It hasn't got a chance,' he announced.

Lawson winced. He had had a wonderful career. As a young man he stood at the right hand of Alec Taylor, master of Manton in Leicestershire. It was rather like a subaltern being attached to the staff of Marshal Ney or the Duke of Wellington. One couldn't fail to learn. Taylor was a giant of a trainer. He was a perfectionist whose genius flowered most spectacularly the day his filly Sceptre won the 1903 Jockey Club Stakes. Sceptre, giving 15 lb to Rock Sand, winner of the Two Thousand Guineas, Derby, and St Leger, put in a performance so game, so brilliant that it would always live in the memory of those who saw it.

Every day there was something new to learn at Manton and Lawson absorbed the lessons well. When Taylor retired in 1927 Lawson took over, and by 1931 he had mastered the art of preparing racehorses so well that his season's winnings totalled £93,899. It was a staggering achievement, one which was not matched for more than thirty years. Remarkably, the winnings were shared among thirty-four horses. There had been no lucky strike, no vein of gold discovered suddenly in the running of one colt or filly. He had done it along the trying, testing route, by superb judgement of a string's potential and shrewd placement in the most suitable races.

Inevitably Lawson won classics. He produced two excellent colts, Orwell and Court Martial, winners of the 1932 and 1945 Two Thousand Guineas. There had been a stream of good fillies. Pennycomequick won him his first classic, the 1929 Oaks. Exhibitionist picked up the Thousand Guineas and the Oaks, as did Galatea II, in the colours of Robert Sterling Clark. But that was in 1939. There had been no Derby, no super colt, and it nagged Lawson. He had a streak of determination in him which was emphatically displayed when the Manton stables were sold and at an advanced age he moved himself and his horses to Newmarket.

Never Say Die was no super colt, but old Joe Lawson had a feeling, an instinct and he was reluctant to leave his investigation of the colt's potential unconcluded. He was determined that the colt should have a real chance to prove himself. He had seen something – and so had Gerald McElligot, Clark's British racing manager.

Both Lawson and McElligot urged Clark to enter for the Derby. He yielded, but without enthusiasm, and he made no plans for the then arduous flight to England. Clark's lack of enthusiasm – and that of Piggott – was not difficult to understand. Though decently bred (sired by Nasrullah, champion stallion in England in 1951 and third in the 1943 Derby, out of Singing Grass, who was sired by the formidable American horse, War Admiral) Never Say Die had been a plodding two-year-old in good company. There had been one victory, in the six-furlong Rosslyn Stakes at Ascot, but in five other outings he had been unable to produce anything better than two third places, and on these occasions he was beaten by horses giving him considerable weight advantage.

Why did Joe Lawson nourish his dream of Derby success

on such unpromising horseflesh? He argued that there had been glimmers at the end of the 1953–4 winter. The colt which had appeared so backward in the spring of 1953 was showing some signs. They were not, it should be said, written across the sky over Newmarket Heath, but he had been putting in some good gallops and he ran decently in Aintree's Union Jack Stakes at the start of the 1954 flat season. Though Piggott was somewhat unimpressed by Never Say Die's performance that day – he finished behind Tudor Honey despite being 5 lb better off – the colt started favourite for the Free Handicap.

If Piggott had been less than enchanted at Aintree his mood was positively sour after the Free Handicap. Never Say Die never acted, never threatened, and finished well down the field. Manny Mercer rode him in his next race, the Newmarket Stakes. He had been considered something of a hot thing in the Free Handicap. At Newmarket he was cold and 20–1. The race was won by Elopement, who was half a length in front of Golden God. Never Say Die was third, a further head away. This would not appear to be the great signal Joe Lawson had been so patiently awaiting over a year of broken hopes but it was after the Newmarket Stakes that Lawson argued for a Derby challenge and McElligot, the racing manager, backed him. The thread of logic might be fine, but it could be traced and both men felt that it would be folly to ignore it.

Their case rested on the premise that this had been a rare occasion when Manny Mercer, the ill-fated brother of 1979 Champion Jockey Joe, had failed to draw out the potential of his horse. Never Say Die's strength, they argued, was his stamina and he had been given no chance of exploiting this by the combination of a slow pace, and Mercer's decision to delay the real challenge to the last moment. When Mercer did make his move it was too sudden, too hectic. The horse had been given no chance to build a winning rhythm. He had been left unbalanced for those crucial seconds when he should have been releasing full power. Lawson made the point that had Never Say Die been given a smoother ride he might be going to Epsom in the same elevated bracket as the joint favourites, Rowston Manor, a northern raider, and the French colt Ferriol.

As it was, Never Say Die would go as a 33–1 shot. But he would go. Joe Lawson set his jaw, firmly adjusted his half-moon spectacles, and considered how best to attract a jockey. There was no great rush to respond to Lawson's call. He put it out that Never Say Die had been performing wonderfully on the gallops, which was not altogether a lie, but in public the colt had run too often without inspiration. Five senior jockeys are said to have turned Lawson down. It had to be young Piggott, decided Lawson.

Part of the trainer's art is feeding into an imaginary computer all the evidence – the hints of weakness, the suggestions of strength – and then acting on the feed-back. The very best trainers are aware that horses can never be machines and the same was true of jockeys, even the relentless, poker-faced young Piggott. Lawson had latched onto a fact which Piggott had concealed from all but his own small circle of family and professional connections: that in the months after the 1952 Derby Piggott had been consumed with an ever-increasing guilt about his performance on Gay Time.

The more Piggott thought about it the more he convinced himself that he should have outridden Charlie Smirke on Tulyar. Years later Piggott admitted to the late Jack Wood:

I shall never forgive myself for losing that Derby. Smirke won the race on Tulyar and he kidded everyone that he won easily. But had I not been so young, had not so many things gone wrong, Charlie would never have made his famous 'What did I Tulyar' remark as he dismounted.

Charlie was a showman, a bit of a Cassius Clay, but a great rider. Although I had ridden my first winner four years earlier, I was still a kid and after Gay Time had lost a shoe, I felt oddly nervous as I went down to the start after all the others. We did not get away as we should have done and my horse did not have enough pace to get up with the leaders, which is essential going into Tattenham Corner. I did not give the colt the right sort of race. I was, I suppose, a little raw. The race calls for guts as well as skill. The stretch after the winning-post is the most dangerous in the world. The last straw on Gay Time came when he pitched on his nose when we reached the road by the big pub. Maybe it was his way of telling me I had ridden a stinker.

Piggott raw? It is hard to imagine now. Whatever the validity of his guilt, Piggott's other kind of rawness, that sore feeling which comes to any professional when he believes he has left some unfinished business, was shrewdly exploited by Lawson. The old trainer sent Piggott a telegram which gambled heavily on the rawness of the young jockey outweighing a certain arrogance of opinion: 'You ride Never Say Die. Still feel sore about losing on Gay Time to Smirkie?' Although Piggott's opinion of Never Say Die had not noticeably improved, he bit on the implications of the telegram. He agreed to ride Never Say Die, even though he was to advise his parents on the drive from Lambourn to Epsom that they should expect nothing. 'No chance', he repeated.

Derby Day 1954 was as unpromising as young Piggott's mood. Sir Winston Churchill was wrapped up against the cold, as was the young Queen, who came to cheer her colt Landau. The sky was grey, the wind was cold, and the country was changing. Sir Winston Churchill's leadership was being challenged; he was at last beginning to tire of government. It was just as well there was a Derby to take a chap's mind off things.

Piggott walked briskly into the paddock. He was wearing the cerise and grey colours of Robert Sterling Clark, who at that time was watching the mist clearing from the morning skyline of Manhattan. At that moment Clark had no particular urge to swap Central Park for the downs, to journey three thousand miles for a place in the paddock among the lovely colts, their coats shining like burnished silk. It wasn't that he didn't relish all that. He was a committed Anglophile who was later that summer to perform an act of gallantry which Sir Walter Raleigh would have found hard to beat: he withdrew his horses when it became clear that he was the only rival to the Queen's chances of winning the Owners' Championship. The problem about Clark's enthusiasm for the 1954 Derby was that he had always been a winner. He had made his fortune through the Singer sewing-machine company and as a sportsman and a breeder he set himself the most demanding standards. Following a dispute with the US racing authorities he announced coolly that never again would one of his horses race on American soil. No one doubted that he meant it, nor was surprised when he followed through. The thought of travelling to Epsom with a reasonable hope of success simply did not appeal. He was a product of American business and sport, where the concept of smiling in defeat runs about level with drive-in croquet. His brother Ambrose was also a formidable sportsman and breeder, having twice won the Grand National.

As Piggott took Never Say Die up to the parade before the grandstand, and then the canter round to the start, it seemed to him that the 5–1 joint favourites Rowston Manor and Ferriol were likely to come under pressure from at least three challengers carrying superior credentials to his own colt. There was Darius, son of Dante and already the winner of the Two Thousand Guineas priced at 7–1; Elopement, winner of the Newmarket Stakes, and partnered by the Epsom specialist Smirke; and Blue Sail, a colt owned by a Canadian oil millionaire and ridden by the celebrated American Johnny Longden.

The best you could say of Never Say Die through the lengthy ritual which goes before the start was that he looked powerful enough, the blaze head seemed calm and there was no hint of agitation or lather. That Piggott sat coolly aboard went without comment. Joe Lawson walked back up to the grandstand. He had done all that he could. He had secured a good rider. He had kept faith with this quirkish animal, followed the classic, time-tested pattern.

Now he simply had to take up the binoculars, control the nerves, and hope that when the great cavalry charge came skimming across the shoulder of the downs and dipped into Tattenham Corner, he would see the blaze of Never Say Die and Piggott, in cerise and grey silks, moving smoothly into prominence. He did. His grip tightened on the binoculars. There was thunder in his ears and his old heart prepared to pound.

Never Say Die had moved powerfully at the start,

Piggott feeling a surge of anticipation as the colt, unlike Gay Time two years earlier, found no difficulty in gaining good ground in the bunch which attached itself to the heels of the early leader L'Avengro. The pursuers were predictable. There was Rowston Manor, hinting at unlimited power. There was Willy Snaith on the Queen's Landau. There was Manny Mercer, hopefully keeping something up his sleeve on Darius. There was Charlie Smirke scenting a new Derby triumph on Elopement. There was Blue Sail and Johnny Longden, a long way from the flat circular tracks of Southern California but, for the moment, at least, coping well enough.

Smirke, Piggott's tormentor of two years previously, lost it going down to Tattenham Corner, and said later, 'I couldn't believe it. He didn't gallop down the hill. He just fell down it.' Rowston Manor and Landau had displaced L'Avengro by the corner and they entered a short fierce duel into the straight. But they couldn't shake off Darius or Never Say Die. At three furlongs Rowston Manor blew a gasket. At two the same thing happened to Landau. Patriotic noises were strangled in thousands of throats. There was no sight of Rae Johnstone's fancied French contender Ferriol. He had thrown in the towel after a mile.

Joe Lawson's heart pounded now. His colt was taking it up two furlongs out from the Derby finishing post. This was the big one after fifty years. This was Lester Piggott, the kid he had coaxed into riding this Derby, thrusting Never Say Die into the rising ground and there was Darius and Manny Mercer failing to mount a challenge. Arabian Night, another 33–1 outsider, was finishing sharply but had too much ground to make. Piggott sat still. Even his elbows were fixed. He won by two lengths.

Keith Piggott describes the mood of his son during the car ride home to Lambourn after the first Derby win:

Really I think he was very elated, but he never showed his feelings about anything. He was pleased because he had worked so very hard for every bit of success he had. I think it hurt him when he got the impression that some people thought he was a bit of an upstart, a kid who was maybe in too much of a hurry. He knew how many hours he had put in to get where he was. He felt deep down that he deserved his success.

After the race there was no sign that Lester Piggott believed he had crossed a great demarcation line in his career and his life. But it was true. He had crowned the most spectacular entry into racing since sixteen-year-old Frankie Wootton became champion jockey in 1903. Piggott had become the youngest jockey to win the Derby. Not until a boy called Steve Cauthen came galloping out of Kentucky more than twenty years later would the world of racing know anything as remotely dramatic as the poise of this pale-faced youngster who stood outside the jockeys' room at Epsom and announced in his matter-of-fact way: 'Never Say Die went well according to plan. Unlike Gay Time he was able to keep up with the leaders. I had some luck. I had a comfortable ride. I feel pleased.'

He might have been talking about a maiden race at Salisbury.

In New York Robert Sterling Clark sat up in bed and said, 'I'm flabbergasted.' Three hours later he said: 'I still haven't gotten over it. I still can't believe it.' But soon a mood of celebration set in. He fired off a barrage of transatlantic cables. To Lawson, to McElligot, to Piggott, and also to the Earl of Rosebery. 'Good families live long' was his jaunty message to the great patron of the turf. It was a reference to the fact that Never Say Die was related, through third dam Galaday, to one of the Rosebery bloodstock lines.

The only thing Robert Sterling Clark couldn't do was lead the colt into the winners' enclosure and order up the bubbly. He had thought often about the pleasure of leading in a Derby winner. Never Say Die was the first American-bred to win the Derby since Iroquois in 1881, the first American-owned winner since 1914. And here he was, the great sportsman Robert Sterling Clark, sitting in a nursing home in the concrete canyons of Manhattan on a day when cheers had rolled across the downs for his colt – and his owner's rights had been assumed by a stable-lad in the winners' enclosure.

He summoned his secretary and delivered brusque orders. 'Make arrangements for a trip to England,' he said.

For the racing crowd Derby night usually offers an exhaustive round of parties. The fashionable parts of London are dotted with racing binges. One such bash was staged by Max Bell, owner of Blue Sail, at the Savoy. It had been conceived, like many of these parties, as a great celebration. This one proved an interesting experiment in how much concentrated gloom could be generated by six hundred guests gathered in a brilliantly-lit room and invited to take supper of caviare and the very best champagne.

Maurice Winnick's band tried gamely to inject a hint of brio. But it is not that easy whooping it up without a twinge when you know that your host has just been thwarted in one of the great ambitions of his life. The Marquis of Milford Haven and Gilbert Harding arrived. Perhaps unsurprisingly, neither of them was able to relieve the gloom of the Canadian oil man. The jockey Longden, who had known so much success in the United States, told a dwindling, fidgety circle that when he had 'stepped on the gas' at Tattenham Corner 'there was just not a damn thing left'. He turned to his blonde wife and said, 'Never mind, honey, we will come back and win.' They never did.

Before Maurice Winnick's band took its first break Joe Lawson was back in his study in Newmarket. He sipped his nightcap, rolled it round his mouth and enjoyed the flavour. There was a sharp pleasure in the oil paintings of the great horses. It had been a wonderful road from Manton to Newmarket. He thought of his day as Alec Taylor's travelling head lad. He thought of all the wins and losses, the lost sheep, the miles covered, the ups and the downs that had shaped him and delivered him to this evening of great triumph. Now there was just one more prize left. It was the St. Leger, the last great goal of the English flat season. He could win that one, too, in the autumn. This time, he thought with a new sharp pleasure, he would not have to cajole and coax a rider on to the back of Never Say Die. There might even be enthusiasm from young Piggott.

Dusk was falling over Manhattan as Maurice Winnick's

men struck up again beneath the chandeliers. Robert Sterling Clark looked out at the mid-town neon and felt the same surge of pleasure which lapped round Joe Lawson in the softly lit Newmarket study. The old men were doing something that life teaches all those who have waged many campaigns. They were celebrating their victory, drawing from it all the heady sap that comes with the knowledge that you have had a great triumph.

Lester Piggott was asleep. He rose to greet the Berkshire dawn. He went about his work. Perhaps he sensed he had to pace himself in the matter of celebrating great victories. He knew there would be more.

5 The Waiting Game

Joe Lawson relaxed in the morning sunshine. It changed everything. Never Say Die, going for his last prize, had been given more than a reprieve. There was nothing to stop the Derby winner now. He would have floundered on soft going over the St Leger's one and three quarter mile course. On the eve of the classic Lawson had looked up at the swollen clouds scudding over Doncaster's Town Moor course and said: 'This is a tragedy.' He was given to such language; racing had invaded every corner of his life. He went on glumly: 'It's all against Never Say Die now.' There was no argument. The price drifted overnight.

But the morning was crisp, the going would be good. Never Say Die would come home a winner and there would be no tightening of the binoculars this time. He would win it by twelve lengths. The jockey in the cerise and grey silks would mock the rest of the field on the run-in. He would stand up in the stirrups, flaunt his vast lead. Robert Sterling Clark, the owner, would continue to defy doctors' orders and rush to greet his victorious colt.

And what of Lester Piggott? He would listen to Never Say Die's triumph on his car radio. He had been water-skiing at Ruislip Lido.

Any analysis of the character of Lester Piggott, his attitude to authority and the world, would be incomplete without careful consideration of this bizarre fact. Piggott, of course, did not water-ski at Ruislip out of choice. His triumph at Epsom had scarcely cooled when he was thrown out of racing for six months; when a world built with such frenzied application was simply knocked down, bulldozed into a pile of rubble on the stable-yard.

We know that in Piggott's early years admiration for his progress and his courage had been tempered with concern that his style might veer to the reckless, that in a straight choice between risking his neck, and those of his rivals, and driving in a winner the chance of the more cautious option prevailing was remote. But no one was prepared for the savage repercussions of his first outing with Never Say Die after the Derby win. It came in the King Edward VII Stakes, one of the great showpieces of the racing calendar and Royal Ascot. Piggott was thrust into the dock on a charge of reckless riding. He found difficulty in striking a note of penance. It had been a rough race, one that sent gasps heaving through the crowds. Never Say Die had been in the thick of it, finished unplaced, and Piggott was called to the Stewards. He was told that he would be stood down for the rest of the meeting. He was also told that a report would be going to the Jockey Club Stewards. Piggott suffered a massive attack of internal seething. So did his father.

What they could not know was that their first bitter reactions would be soon overtaken, engulfed even, by a new level of rage. The word from the Jockey Club (racing's ruling body) made Ascot's summary justice seem something close to benevolence. Lester Piggott, said the Jockey Club, would be banned for six months and he would also have to leave his father's home, attach himself to another trainer. He would have to pack his bags and turn his back on Lambourn, the springboard of all his success, and take up work as a stable-lad. It was rather as if the young and errant George Best had been told, shortly after scoring a goal in the European Cup, that he must play for a Sunday League team. Worse still, Piggott could not do the equivalent of kicking a ball away from his own stable-yard and gallops, which were to be Jack Jarvis's at Newmarket.

By any standards it was an odd affair and even now, twenty-six years later, it is not easy disentangling the arguments, the hurts, claims and counter-claims. The Piggotts, perhaps not surprisingly, still feel somewhat bitter when the subject is raised. Sir Gordon Richards, who some people felt was at least as guilty as Piggott, is vague: 'It's all a long time ago and the incident happened so quickly. It seemed that Lester was trapped in a pocket, went for daylight, and the result was a series of bumps. I wouldn't like to be categorical.'

The Times reported the race in typically unadorned style.

The King Edward VII Stakes caused the crowd to gasp twice. As the horses came round the turn into the straight, Rashleigh (Sir G. Richards) and Garter (W. Rickaby) received bumps which nearly put them on the floor. Never Say Die, with L. Piggott up, had been pocketed on the outside of these two. Half-way up the straight Blue Prince II and Arabian Night were racing together in front. Arabian Night crossed rather quickly from the outside position to the rails, and a moment later swerved right out towards Blue Prince II again. Meanwhile Sir Gordon Richards on Rashleigh, pursued by Tulyar's brother, Tarjoman, came up on the outside to win.

The immediate behaviour of the Ascot stewards was as erratic as the running of the big race. First, they objected to Rashleigh. Then they withdrew their objection and hauled in Piggott. Justice was seen to wobble rather than be done when, finally, the Jockey Club announced that they

. . . had taken notice of his dangerous and erratic riding both this season and in previous seasons and that in spite of continuous warnings he continued to show complete disregard for the Rules of Racing and the safety of other jockeys. Before any application for a renewal of Piggott's licence can be entertained he must be attached to some other trainer other than his father for a period of six months.

He went to Jarvis, taking lodgings with his uncle, ex-jockey Fred Lane. It was not like being banished to Siberia. In Newmarket, headquarters of racing, Piggott was tantalizingly close to many of the finest horses in England, horses he would have been riding at the great meetings, but for the arbitrary decision made by a group of elderly men sitting in a musty committee-room far from the heat of action. He rode at work some excellent horses. He felt the wonderful sensation of striking a good, rhythmic gallop. But there was nothing at the end of it, none of the intoxicating ritual which had carried him from the jockeys' room to the paddock and the start, and then the great tingle of the off, when the adrenalin flowed and life became a wonderfully simple matter of being first past the finishing-post.

In the first bleak days of his sentence Piggott was inconsolable. He had told the stewards that he thought their decision unfair and 'ridiculously harsh'; from such a taciturn youth this was a statement of some high emotion. After coming away from the stewards his assessment of the situation was blunt: 'Six months bloody hard labour and less than a fiver a week while serving it.'

Later, long after his blood had cooled, he gave his own version of the affair.

The colt [Never Say Die] was a much better performer on a left-hand course like Epsom but he had handled Ascot's right-hand turns quite well. When we got near home I felt sure we would win. My cousin Bill Rickaby was to the left on Garter and I could see that he was on a beaten horse. I made a move outwards and at the same time Gordon made his effort on Rashleigh. He was on the outside with Garter in the middle of the sandwich. There is still no doubt all this long time after that Gordon's horse bumped Garter on to me. As always he was desperately keen to win and Never Say Die was the chief sufferer. I lost momentum just as I was picking my horse up for the finish and the bump put us out of the race. Gordon went on to win and we finished fourth. I was called in by the stewards. It was a bit like a court-martial and they stood me down for the rest of the afternoon. I was the bad boy but a lot of people thought Rashleigh should have been disqualified. I'm convinced that had the camera patrol been in operation then as it is today the stewards must have stood Gordon down as well. There was nothing dangerous in what I did.

The words are restrained enough but it is not difficult to guess at the depth of feelings which generated them. Keith Piggott, who fought to restrain his own anger and disgust when the stewards told him they were doing all this for his boy's own good, said, 'Lester is heart-broken. His whole life is racing. But I keep telling him that six months will seem nothing when compared with his tremendous future in the game'. Now Keith Piggott is less diplomatic.

The further we get away from the whole affair the more people come to the conclusion that Lester was given a raw deal. There was a lot of jealousy among some of the older jockeys, you know. They had a feeling that Lester was coming in and taking rides that should have been theirs. Frankly, some of them were past it, they were just hanging on and here was Lester just coming into the business and really looking like a winner. He was going for every chance. He was doing what every good jockey should, giving his horses every chance to win. It wasn't that he was dangerous. You can't eliminate danger from racing, anyway. It was simply that he was young and brave and that there was nothing wrong with his nerve. Maybe his nerve shocked a few people. Perhaps it was something they couldn't quite understand in someone so young. I could understand it. It thrilled me, this knowledge about my son's talent and I just hoped that he wouldn't become bitter and disillusioned over what happened to him after the Ascot race. In fact I need not have worried. He knuckled down at Jack Jarvis's. He had good horses to ride and he knew I was working hard to get him back before the six months were up. Some people argue that the break did him good, made him learn a little bit of patience, but I can't be sure about that at all. I don't think there is any way you can justify something that is basically unfair, and nothing will persuade me that what happened to my boy was anything other than a terrible piece of injustice. I'm also convinced that come what may, Lester would have been a great jockey. He didn't need six months in the cooler to help him to that achievement. The thing that consoles me is that if it didn't do him any good it certainly didn't do him any harm – not in the long run anyway.

But it is of course, a long, long time from June even to September, which was when Piggott senior finally prevailed on the authorities to lift their ban. Clearly there had been time enough for the Jockey Club stewards to ponder the validity of their judgement and the decision to relent three months early might be seen as something of a comment on their original decision. The stewards had one last reservation, however: they made sure that Piggott's licence was withheld until after the St Leger.

Piggott had from the start of the suspension buried himself in the timeless rituals of the business. There were inevitably bad days; days when the sense of injustice refused to be subdued. He felt like a highly-trained fighter kicking his heels back in garrison. There was one day when the rub and the irritation lowered his spirits, made him vulnerable. Here was a star, a Derby winner, working as a stable-lad and it may have been that the incongruity of it all swept over him when a 62-year-old stable-lad asked him brusquely about the whereabouts of a pair of grooming brushes. There was an incident, the police were called, and the stable-lad, Peter Kearns, finished up in hospital with an ear injury.

From hospital, Kearns said: 'I had attended to one of my horses and when I went to do the other I couldn't find my grooming brushes. I spoke to young Piggott about them. He made me so angry I clipped him one. I have told the police that.' As Kearns gave his version it was noted that he was wearing a large dressing on his left ear.

When Piggott spoke of the incident he had a vivid bruise beneath his eye. Pointing to the bruise, he said:

> This – it was a lot worse a few days ago – and a cut inside my lip were what Kearns did to me. It was just bad luck that his ear was cut so badly; he stumbled and hit his ear on the concrete. I didn't mean to hurt him – I was just defending myself. I had finished grooming one of my horses and later, putting my tools away, I must have taken Kearns' instead. He came storming up. I said I must have put them in the saddle room by mistake. He went to the wrong saddle room, then came back in a temper and hit me and I cut my lip. I didn't want any trouble with a man so much older so I walked away. He came after me and hit me again. I told him not to be so daft over a thing like that, but he still wanted to fight and it was then that I hit him. He got up bleeding. I wanted to shake hands but he still wanted to fight. I pushed him away. Then he went off to the police. Now I'm hoping that this will blow over without spoiling my chances of riding again.

He was obsessively concerned that he might fall foul of some conspiracy which would keep him from fulfilling his destiny as a great rider. He emerged unscathed from the incident, however, and went back to work with the mental note that no detail, not even a grooming brush, was too small to ignore.

Some Piggott-watchers were impressed with his demeanour. His scuffle with the elderly stable-lad can be seen as a rare lapse in control. Harry Carr, the ex-royal jockey, said:

> It was terribly hard for him at first. You see, he was already one of the greats. He had made his way among the top jockeys and it was as though he had been slapped down, pushed right back to square one. I suppose you have to wonder whether it would break his spirit. But no. All of us who came into regular contact with him were surprised at the way he buckled down to the life of a stable-lad. It was as though he was saying nothing would stop him.

It was ironic that the man Joe Lawson chose to replace Piggott for the St Leger was Charlie Smirke. 'Smirkie' had fired so much of Piggott's determination in the summer of Never Say Die. His smooth piloting of Tulyar to Derby success had been both an example and a reproach to the young rider. Smirke was master of his trade and in the 1952 Derby he had seemed to embody all the qualities Piggott was eagerly seeking to evolve in his own technique. Considering his own feeling that had he been smarter he would have denied Smirke his success on Tulyar, and that he was losing a chance to carry off two classics in his nineteenth year, Piggott showed a certain generosity of spirit. He rang Charlie Smirke to advise him on the riding of Never Say Die, giving him a precise breakdown on the way the colt had performed in the Derby. Smirke, a marvellously gifted rider with much subtlety and flair, appreciated the call and was impressed by the boy's feel for the subject. If Piggott's telephone manner was somewhat brusque the content was a model of clarity.

Piggott was invited to Doncaster but there was a limit to his ability to control his frustrations in public. Instead he tried to shut the St Leger from his mind. He water-skied at Ruislip and, although it was a sparkling day and the newly-discovered sport exhilarating, his search for detachment was only partly successful. The thought of Doncaster still nagged him; *he* should be hearing the muffled thunder of the crowd rather than Smirkie.

He returned to his car and turned on the radio in time for the off. It was a formal victory for Smirke, who had Never Say Die last of the sixteen-strong field over the first two furlongs. Smirke was fifteen lengths behind By Thunder and Double Bore as he brought Never Say Die along on the outside coming into the straight. Smoothly he moved to the rail, all the time feeling the gathering power of Never Say Die. It is a wonderful feeling, jockeys say. It is the feeling you might get stepping into a classic car and discovering that you have power, real power totally under your control. Smirke hit the front three furlongs out. 'I had a perfect run through,' he said afterwards, 'and was cantering over them when I made my challenge on the inside.' Robert Sterling Clark exclaimed: 'Gee, have I got a horse.'

Lester Piggott flicked off the car radio and drove away from Ruislip Lido. He never met Robert Sterling Clark, who died two years later, a happy man. He had presented Never Say Die to the National Stud, a gesture which nicely captured the old man's feeling for England and his appreciation of the fact that the old country had provided him with a superb climax to his days in racing. In the aftermath of the St Leger win Clark had long talks with Joe Lawson. The old trainer was saddened by Clark's decision to retire the horse. 'I think it is a tragedy. I have tried everything to persuade Mr Clark to keep the horse in training.' There was some poignancy in Lawson's statement. He, too, was nearing the end of his life. Right at the end of his career the great elusive goal had been achieved. He had found a colt to dominate an English summer. He was reluctant to let it go.

For Piggott, of course, time had been suspended, and for not as long he had originally imagined. His father's campaigning, which had been quiet but persistent, and his own stoic demeanour had had an effect at the Jockey Club.

The lifting of the ban – on 23 September 1954, eleven days after the St Leger – was both a sharp pleasure and a shock. It left him, for one of the few occasions of his life, unprepared to go out to ride a winner. His weight had gone up to 9 st 7 lb. He had to shed a stone and a half in five days. He did it, of course. He recalled: 'My weight had gone up terribly. I hardly ate a thing for five days. I ran dozens of miles.'

It was his first bout of sustained, desperate wasting and it tested the extent of his will-power. He was getting a savage foretaste of the years of his maturity, when all colour would leave his cheeks and when, more than most men, he could give some insight into his concept of purgatory. But he never questioned whether it was worth it; it was simply something that had to be done. In the glow of an autumn day at Newmarket he returned a winner, riding Cardington King home in the first race. He was cheered all the way. Piggott remembers being surrounded by well-wishers, some of whom had not been quite so visible in the months of exile.

People started saying that my lay-off had done me good. But I cannot think that it did. The talks I had with those closest to me had some effect and maybe when I went back I was a little more wary because any further trouble might have seen me suspended for life. But after five years I was already maturing, anyway. I still ride the same way. I still take chances and I can honestly say I have never been frightened. If I ever felt that way I would give up. Racehorses travel up to forty miles an hour and the game isn't one for anyone who gets scared.

Looking back, it is easy to see that the summer of 1954 was a vital phase of Lester Piggott's life. It was a microcosm of his career. There was the poise and the fire of his Derby win. There was the bitter taste of Royal Ascot, the growing awareness that his methods and nature would inexorably take him into prolonged conflict with authority. There was the wasting, the agony and the resilience which would become part of his life, reinforce the contours of his personality. There was the frustration reflected in the scuffle with the elderly stable-lad. And at the end of it there was the slightly grudging recognition that in Piggott there was, perhaps, a unique talent.

The recognition which mattered most came from one of the great trainers of all time. Noel Murless announced that his jockey Sir Gordon Richards had decided to retire and his successor would be Lester Piggott. Murless had no need to elaborate; with that decision he produced a volume of comment.

6 Safety in Numbers

Piggott, Lawson and Clark was a happy accident, a firm that sprang up by chance and dissolved as quickly and as haphazardly as it was formed. Piggott, Murless and Sassoon was something different. It was, in the end, almost a case for the Monopoly Commission. In some ways they were birds of a feather, in others their plumage contrasted sharply. Piggott, the boy born to ride, came to racing as a son of a blacksmith might go to the anvil. Murless chose the world of racing although easily able to follow an academic or military career with success. Sir Victor Sassoon came to the turf in search of diversion, to find colour and glory away from the mills of industry and the great banking houses. Sir Victor was fabulously rich and schooled in the ways of the English aristocracy. The similarities were a deep love of fine horseflesh, an endless need to achieve perfection, and natures which were shut off from close inspection.

Piggott guessed at the strength of the combination when he drove up to Warren Place, Newmarket, in 1954. He was still some weeks from his nineteenth birthday but already the power groups and nuances of racing were at his fingertips, as they were to remain throughout his career. In later years obscure trainers would be stunned and dazzled by telephone calls from the great Piggott, suggesting he ride one of their contenders at, say, Chepstow next Tuesday. His command of the game was to become encyclopaedic.

Piggott's journey up the hill to Warren Place was not entirely by invitation. The truth was he had fashioned the meeting as smoothly as some old political wheeler-dealer might organize a caucus in a backroom at Westminster.

Of course Murless knew about Piggott; he had watched the young jockey's progress. However, there was a whole academy to choose from and Murless was offering something rather more than another job. Piggott described his decision in his classic deadpan manner, shrugging off suggestions that it might have been slightly forward to ring up a man of Murless's calibre and say, in effect, 'I'm prepared to ride for you.' When Piggott made the call he was still under suspension. He took the initiative straight after talking to Sir Gordon Richards, who wanted to sign Piggott for his own venture into training.

I was flattered by Sir Gordon's offer. At least it killed those stories that Gordon and I didn't get on. But I knew Mr Murless was looking for a first jockey and I called him. It was a call which changed my life. All sorts of famous names were being linked with the big stable at Warren Place. Mr Murless asked me to go and see him. We fixed a very worthwhile retainer and in the winter of 1954 I began to ride work for him. Within weeks I realized what a wonderful job I had landed.

It is staggering to think of Piggott's nerve at that age. At Sir Gordon Richards's retirement party at the Savoy he and Piggott were photographed together, the master and he apprentice. Piggott, drinking fruit juice, looks self-conscious and shy, slightly in awe of Sir Gordon, celebrating with champagne. Within weeks of that party Piggott was turning down an offer from the great man.

Piggott says that he knew 'within weeks' that the move to Murless was a good one. Beyond the merest shadow of a doubt, Piggott knew it even as he came up the road winding between the gallops and swung left into Warren Place. Murless's house and stables invariably had an extraordinary effect on the visitor. He had bought Warren Place and its eleven acres from John D. Clark, a Wimbledon surveyor and financier, in 1952. The previous owner was the Maharanee of Baroda. The house was certainly a place for the illustrious. Going up to Warren Place is like entering the very canvas and oils of a fine old English landscape painting. The gallops are of a lustrous green, the horses gleam in the morning sunlight. Piggott had only to look around to know that his career, after all the dramatic surges and lurches, had entered a new phase. The setting of his work was superb.

Warren Place throbbed with efficiency, though the noise of it was not intrusive. Murless's staff operated on a basis of permanent alert. Piggott's new trainer was a man whose professional excellence was acknowledged in every corner of the game. His principal owner, Sassoon, had a passion for the turf and a grandeur of will that meant he would devote endless resources, both of finance and imagination, to the pursuit of glory.

Piggott's first impression of Murless was comical.

> His hat was one of the oldest I had seen. I'm sure someone had broken it in for him. And as he led his huge string on to the heath I looked at his enormous feet and felt happy that I would never have to ride against him. For I thought that what looked like size 27s would only have to be turned upwards [*sic*] in the stirrups to make it impossible for anyone to pass him.

Tall, straight and courtly, Murless was as unaffected as the hat suggested. Even at the height of his power, when everyone wanted to shake his hand and pat his back, he recoiled from the throng of a great race-meeting. He said that caring for horses, sitting astride his hack – which for a time was the great, sad steeplechaser Devon Loch – was everything, and that the celebrity of being a master trainer was, by comparison, nothing. His study, a homely, cluttered room, was adorned with portraits of his beloved horses. But he exerted intense discipline and would be enraged by an apparently trivial misdemeanour. Once, Geoff Lewis recalls, a stable-lad had worked sloppily in one of the boxes. Murless dismissed him on the spot and then swirled off to his breakfast. The sacked stable-lad was lingering, downcast, in the yard when Murless returned. 'I told you to get out,' said Murless. 'I hoped you might reconsider, sir,' said the stable-lad. The great trainer relented and put the stable-lad back to work. That evening a knock came to Murless's door. It was the stable-lad. He wondered if he might borrow the cost of a deposit on a motor bike. He got it.

It was a strange mingling of strength and softness, but temperamental inconsistency paled against an overwhelming quality: his highly-developed instinct for the potential of a racehorse and the various strengths and weaknesses of its nature. At the time of his knighthood in Jubilee Year Murless said of himself, 'If I had a secret it might be that I have let the horses guide me. I have always seen them as flesh and blood – not machines. I have perhaps respected their moods – and understood their problems.'

Charles Francis Noel Murless was born in Malpas, Cheshire, in 1910 and by the age of four he, like Lester Piggott, had made irreversible contact with the equine world. The object of his affection, and his fascination, was a Welsh pony called Mary Jane. Murless recalls:

> My father was away at the war and my mother was also away, nursing. There wasn't anyone much left at home to talk to and live with except the little Welsh pony. She gave me my first knowledge about life, character and emotion. She gave me that thing called horse sense – an indefinable quality. My parents sent me to public school but I left at sixteen to be a stable-lad for Frank Hartigan at Weyhill in Hampshire. I only wanted to be among horses.

In Hampshire his knowledge and his enthusiasm gathered pace quickly. He had ridden point-to-point in his early teens and those first impressions of jockeyship were measured and tested by his contact at Weyhill with the Hartigan jockeys Steve Donoghue and Gordon Richards. In the thirties he set up a training establishment near Thirsk, Yorkshire, and for years the hierarchy of southern trainers warily eyed the slightly solemn young man from the North.

His most significant training feat, at least in its effect on the shaping of his career, came at Goodwood in 1947. His Closeburn, putting up 8 st 10 lb – a record for a three-year-old at that time – carried the Stewards Cup brilliantly. The great Fred Darling, rainer of seven Derby winners, was on the point of quitting his Beckhampton stables. He was looking for a successor, and Murless had long impressed him.

Darling had noted the turn-out of the Murless horses, the way they were beautifully prepared for important races. It was the work of something more than a good trainer. Fred Darling merely needed a nudge from Gordon Richards. The jockey told him that, in his opinion, the condition of Closeburn represented a perfect feat of training. Fred Darling had found his successor.

In 1948 Murless was England's leading trainer. His Queenpot carried the Thousand Guineas. In 1949 his Ridge Wood took the St Leger. In the years to his retirement Murless was to match Darling. He equalled his number of classic wins (nineteen), and his final total of winners was to be 1,430 with total prize money of £2.6 million. It was a glorious career by any standards and it was in this pale, remote teenager, Lester Piggott, that the full maturity of a training genius was to be entrusted.

Sir Noel recently described his confidence in Piggott in 1954 and the young jockey's bold overture, remembering his reaction to this fine piece of temerity with some amusement:

> We reached a mutual agreement. He made it clear he wanted to work for me. I had been studying some possible replacements for Gordon and it was no easy chore. When Lester Piggott joined me I knew he was not yet a Gordon Richards. How could he be? How could he have gathered together all the knowledge and the experience which Gordon had acquired down all those years? But I knew that Lester Piggott would come to it. Why was I so sure? Well, there were so many things. For a start you only had to look at him with a horse to know that he was a natural horseman. He seemed to reach an understanding with any animal he came across. It was such a rapid thing. Amazing, really. And above all there was his extraordinary ability to ride a finish. He could sit so still, and when he needed to drive home a horse he did it with such marvellous timing.

The question of whether Piggott was a cruel jockey, whether he abused horses in pursuit of victories is obviously a painful one to Sir Noel, who would have traded all the silver trophies of the turf rather than see a horse he loved suffer. At various times the RSPCA and members of the public have made the charge with some vehemence.

Lester Piggott would not have worked for me so long if he had been cruel to horses. I would never pay that price to win a horse race. There is not one worth it. Lester Piggott used the whip when necessary, but he never did it gratuitously, he never did it to punish. He had a great talent for knowing when a horse had something more to give and could be reminded of the job at hand.

Murless had to debate this very problem when he took on Piggott. Some owners already felt that Piggott was free with the whip. They saw his need to win spilling over into a ruthless disregard for the spirit of their expensive horseflesh. Murless's decision had some influence in discrediting their fears.

Sir Victor Sassoon formed the second part of this formidable trinity when Murless moved from Beckhampton to Newmarket. He placed twelve horses with Murless, as did Aly Khan.

The Sassoon fortune was first built in Baghdad, when opium trading was not inconsistent with a place among the city elders. In 1830 the family moved east to Bombay, where in 1867 Sassoon's grandfather, Elias David, set up a banking house. The Sassoon tentacles stretched further east to Shanghai, and then swung west to Basra. When Mao's Red Army came back from the hills and took control of China the Sassoons were said to have lost £7 million. But the family was majestically defended against such pinpricks.

Sir Victor inherited £15 million along with a baronetcy in 1924. He was educated at Harrow and Trinity College, Cambridge. He was a dark, slightly mysterious plutocrat and it was later felt that his character had been sharpened into quirkish angles by a crippling accident sustained in the Royal Flying Corps. Certainly it was a mishap not designed to develop the sunnier side of a man's nature. He was ordered to take part in a fly past despite his insistence that his biplane was unsafe. He trundled off into the sky with extreme reluctance, a tardiness which was entirely justified by the fact that he crashed within minutes, badly crippling his legs. Although he often displayed spectacular acts of generosity (the rescue of the financially embarrassed Steve Donoghue

The fifteen-year-old Lester plays draughts with his father Keith. Iris Piggott picks a winner.

Lester's humour enthralls the stable lads at his father's place in Lambourn.

Some thoughts for a new season: Keith Piggott makes a point to his son, aboard Treize de Sept, on a spring morning on the Berkshire downs.

Lester, aged fourteen, wins his first race as a Senior at Ascot on Tancrad. Suddenly he is someone to look up to, says the glance of apprentice R. Arnold.

Hands firm, seat perfect, Lester could have been one of the great National Hunt jockeys. Here he rides his first hurdle race on Tangle.

Lester, aged eighteen, strides out at York, wearing the Queen's colours.

1954 Derby, the race he was born to win. Lester brings in Never Say Die. Tommy Gosling on Arabian Night and Manny Mercer on Darius follow him home. The feeling would become familiar.

BELOW LEFT Lester is suspended for six months by the Stewards of the Jockey Club. Even when you are ready to take on the world, it is good to have a friend. Lester is comforted by Dominic Forte, apprentice jockey.

BELOW Lester brings in Crepello, his second Derby winner in 1957. Sir Victor Sassoon, owner of the winner, is on the left.

Lester, aged nineteen, drives Wild Knave home at Newbury. Soon he was to abandon National Hunt.

The Aly Khan leads in his winner Petite Etoile after the 1959 Oaks. Piggott and Petite Etoile made poetry in their speed and their understanding.

Lester marries Susan Armstrong, daughter of Newmarket trainer Sam Armstrong. It was his most important engagement that year.

Dawn on the Downs. Lester works out his father's string with Joe McGee.

Lester rolls on the turf before thundering hooves at Brighton. He walked away unaided but, as ever, the margin between glory and disaster was fine.

Lester is banned from the 1962 Derby. No, he doesn't have anything to say; his face tells the story.

Lester wagered that he would have a son, but he paid up happily. His daughter Maureen has become a gifted horsewoman of international recognition.

The face which has been likened to that of a well-kept grave. The great trainer Vincent O'Brien speaks and the great jockey half listens.

Lester was disappointed in Ribofilio but owner Charles Engelhard insisted he tackled the classics. Lester was right.

Piggott pensive. There is always much to consider, to assess and to decide.

There has to be a break: Lester and Susan on the white sands of the Bahamas.

Bottom up all the way. The unique style of the Long Fella. Beyond analysis, beyond imitation, it will go with him when he leaves.

When you spend your life feeding on morsels of chicken and wafers of meat you deserve something of the best....

An appointment with the Queen after winning the King George VI and Queen Elizabeth stakes at Ascot in 1977. The Queen is one of his greatest admirers.

was typical) it seemed that there would always be a residue of bitterness. His mood cannot have been improved by the recurring waves of Indian nationalism which cut across his paternalistic efforts in Indian legislature. He moved to Shanghai.

He bought his first racehorse in 1924, the year of his inheritance. He could no longer dance and play tennis – two youthful passions – and the turf was clearly an alternative relaxation. In 1925 his bloodstock investment was £58,750. His first classic wins came in 1937, Exhibitionist rewarding his heavy outlay of time and money with victories in the Thousand Guineas and the Oaks. At the same time his business activities continued to widen. He set up headquarters in Hong Kong, and then, before the Japanese invasion, moved to the Bahamas. It is hard to imagine a more multinational life, even for a man of such vast energy and financial backing, but the part of the world which drew him most strongly was the green island of the English turf. The fluent speed of a thoroughbred racing in his colours of peacock blue and old gold seemed like a victory over his own disability. The exhilaration lifted him profoundly.

But he was a complex man from a complex background. One day he could perform an act of sweeping charity; he was aware of the plight of his fellow Jews in Nazi Germany, and hundreds of refugees were absorbed into his world-wide empire. But the next day he could penny-pinch as thoroughly as a Lester Piggott perpetuating his own legend. Just after the Second World War, when currency restrictions seemed relentless, a friend asked Sassoon, somewhat desperately, for $3,000 to be paid back in sterling. 'As a banker I cannot agree to that,' said Sassoon, 'but there is nothing to prevent me making a gift.' A member of Sassoon's staff duly arrived at the friend's New York hotel. He had with him $3,000 in traveller's cheques – and a bill for stamp duty. Sassoon stayed in a luxurious suite at the Ritz Hotel, but insisted on laundering his own underwear. When Sir Gordon Richards set up as a trainer he felt confident that Sir Victor would help the launch by sending along a few of his yearlings. He did, after all, breed at least fifty each year at his Newmarket stud. But Sassoon's response to the idea would have been demoralizing to a less confident man than Richards. Sassoon snapped:

'Why should I let a beginner take charge of my horses?'

It was perhaps inevitable that the Sassoon investment of so much cash and time, his insistence on the finest quality of horse and man, would bring him sustained success. He won the 1953 Derby when Richards, to the relief of most of the racing world, brought in Pinza, and it could be sensed then that Sassoon was moving into a period when he would draw huge dividends from his great commitment. Piggott arrived with beautiful timing. He was donning the peacock blue and old gold silks on a flood tide of success. And, of course, Murless had other owners – the Queen and Aly Khan.

In his first year with Murless Piggott had over a hundred winners in 530 rides. Although it was not enough to trouble champion Doug Smith (with 155 winners) Piggott's tally of 103 represented another major stride forward and it was only the splendour of Meld which denied him a second classic success in the St Leger. Meld completed the stunning sweep of the Thousand Guineas and Oaks by relegating Piggott's Nucleus to second place at Doncaster. There was no lack of consolation.

Piggott won the important Eclipse Stakes at Sandown with a beautifully judged race. The Murless–Piggott relationship was flourishing, but not because of any great personal warmth, any mingling of kindred spirits. The basis was pure professionalism and an implicit understanding of the nature and demands of the job. They both had a genius which took them beyond theories and traditions. It was as though they *knew* while many of the others guessed and hoped. They knew horses from their heads to their hooves. And each knew that the other knew, perfectly.

In 1956 Piggott moved up the jockeys' table to third place, pushing his winning total to 129. Doug Smith was still out in front, but Piggott's progress was looking inexorable. 1956 substantial; 1957 would be huge.

7 Cloudless Horizons

The feeling which came to the pit of Lester Piggott's stomach when he first saw Crepello, then later when he sensed the power of the colt beneath him, is one sometimes experienced by lucky art collectors and football scouts. It is part hunch, part observation, part surge of the blood. 'There is something about the looks of a good horse which impresses you,' says Piggott. 'Crepello was a baby when I first saw him and the first work he did stamped him as something special. I got this immediate feeling about him.'

Crepello was a big chestnut baby, the result of careful breeding by Sir Victor Sassoon. He was sired by Donatello II, son of Derby winner Blenheim, and the dam, Crepuscule, also had an impressive sire, Mieuxe, who carried the Prix du Jockey Club and the Grand Prix. The pedigree said that Crepello would be a stayer, perhaps a candidate for the Ascot Gold Cup. But Piggott's excitement about the colt was based on something more tangible. He felt speed. Classic-winning speed.

Therewas, however, a flaw. Crepello rippled with power. He was handsome and big, standing over sixteen hands. He had an impressive body, a fine head with a white blaze – but would this superstructure be successfully carried by those rather straight forelegs? Noel Murless shared Piggott's enthusiasm, sensed, as Joe Lawson had when he first caught sight of Never Say Die, that here might be the end of his long wait for a Derby winner. Murless felt that this colt could win the Derby. But if it was to do so it would have to be nursed carefully along every inch of the road to Epsom.

Murless, as never before, had to justify his reputation for care, patience and superlative timing. He would also have to run a gauntlet of advice and criticism. Secretly he must have felt that some of the advice was impertinent, some of the criticism, at best, ill-informed. At one stage it was even implied that he had lost his grip on the realities of racing, that the gleam of class he saw in Crepello had blinded him to the time-honoured rituals and demands of preparing a Derby horse. Crepello was to go to Epsom lightly raced and much doubted – by those outside of Warren Place.

Piggott's impression of genuine speed was swiftly confirmed. In his first outing, the five-furlong Windsor Castle Stakes at Royal Ascot, Crepello announced his class. Piggott rode nonchalantly. His instructions were simple. He had to let Crepello go at his own pace. He wasn't to apply pressure. If Piggott had only flourished the whip Crepello would have sailed to victory. Instead he finished a close second and vastly enjoyed the afternoon out. Crepello spent the high summer at home in Newmarket.

The wraps came off again in the autumn. Crepello was given a sharpening race, finishing fourth in the Middle Park Stakes. Two weeks later came the Dewhurst Stakes, a race which would largely determine the mood of Warren Place through the winter. Warren Place had a good, optimistic winter. Crepello beat Doutelle in the Dewhurst Stakes by a mere three-quarters of a length, but Piggott felt three-quarters of Crepello's power remained below the surface that autumn afternoon. Piggott reported to Murless that the margin of victory could scarcely have been more deceptive. The victory had been a formality.

'At no stage of the race was there any question in my mind,' said Piggott.

Murless nodded. It was a small, satisfied nod. Later, the trainer admitted that Crepello could have been a giant of a two-year-old: 'He could undoubtedly have won the Champagne Stakes or any of the big two-year-old races.' Later, too, Sir Victor Sassoon revealed how Murless had been in an unusually expansive mood after Crepello's first outing at Royal Ascot.

'He told me then,' recalled Sassoon, 'that Crepello should have just one objective, the Derby. He told me I had bred a Derby winner. He didn't make it sound like speculation.'

But Murless knew he couldn't afford to ignore the hazards. A heavy two-year-old campaign would have exposed those straight forelegs to risk. The dream could suddenly crumble. It would take all of Murless's judgement to negotiate the minefield. Yet it would be worth all the worry, the constant vigilance, to see this lovely chestnut a classic winner. The Derby glittered, a bright light beyond the winter.

Crepello wintered well. He was performing beautifully on the gallops when the hoar-frost gave way to spring. Murless was happy about the colt, but he would have welcomed some spring rain. The air was dry and the ground was hard, risky for a high-class colt with straight forelegs. At the last minute Murless withdrew Crepello from the Blue Riband Trial Stakes at Epsom. It was another cloud across the popular belief in Murless's Derby contender. Murless, said some critics, was throwing away the Two Thousand Guineas. How could you send a colt unraced as a three-year-old to the Guineas? What kind of arrogance was this? It wasn't arrogance, of course. It was a shrewd measurement of the odds, a fine balance between advantage and risk.

The Two Thousand Guineas draw did not favour Piggott. He was on the wide outside. The going was firm. It was as though the fates were giving Piggott, Murless and Sassoon the ultimate in examinations. Crepello was unperturbed, even when Jimmy Eddery, father of Pat, was thrown by Chevastrid. The Irish colt bolted and as handlers vainly tried to bring him under control the delay was calculated to hurt the least experienced contender. Crepello was the only colt unraced as a three-year-old, but he seemed to enjoy the boisterous gathering, and if Piggott was concerned, not a flicker of it showed. He sat still. His face was impassive. In fact, he was running through his mind the strategy that he believed would overcome the disadvantage of the draw. Piggott said that he loved Crepello, felt only a warm surge of affection when he thought of the big chestnut. It was a startling thing for him to say when you remember his earlier pronouncements, particularly his teenage declaration that he saw racehorses as machines, no more, no less. It was a rare confession of an emotion which was first tested and found to be sound that day at Newmarket. Crepello had much to do in the race and every request made of him was answered smartly, without a hint of reluctance. All the way down the Rowley Mile Piggott got to like Crepello a little more.

The chief threat seemed to be Pipe of Peace, ridden by Scobie Breasley, and trained by Sir Gordon Richards. Pipe of Peace started 100–30 favourite and was drawn, like the dangerous northern challenger Quorum, close to Crepello on the outside. Roger Poincelet, riding the formidable French colt Tyrone, might also cause some problems. There was some dismay when Piggott turned down the option of racing along the far rail with Pipe of Peace and Quorum. Instead Piggott tacked across to the stand side, a time-consuming manoeuvre on the wide sweep of the Rowley Mile. Piggott reckoned the gamble was worth it. He wanted Crepello to have plenty of company, plenty of interest.

Crepello's white blaze bobbed at the rear, but he wasn't left behind. Poincelet, after a difficult time at the tapes, had pushed Tyrone to the front and by The Bushes he had shaken off Brioche. But Tyrone seemed short of resolution and by The Dip he was beginning to hang back. Meanwhile Piggott felt the reassurance of a powerful rhythm.

We had crossed to the rails plum last, cantering almly along behind the field. I would see them tiring in front and could feel the beat of Crepello. It was a good feeling. It was unfaltering. We began to pick them off going into The Dip. I really let him go as we hit the rising ground, just as Roger Poincelet brought Tyrone swerving alongside to the right, his whip dangerously close to Crepello's face. Even that did not bother him, and we drew steadily away, easily holding the late challenge of the very useful Quorum.

You might have thought such a victory, perhaps comparable to Blue Peter's Newmarket triumph before the 1939 Derby, would have removed doubts about Crepello's credentials and the handling of his training. Murless, who had previously come close to winning the Two Thousand Guineas with The Cobbler and Abernant, announced that he would bypass the Lingfield Derby trials. His approach to Epsom would continue to be stealthy.

There seemed to be a strange, built-in resistance to the concept of Crepello as a potential superhorse and all the way to Epsom question marks beseiged Warren Place. The most bizarre rumours appeared less than a week before the big race. Speculation that something had 'gone wrong' with Crepello swept through the Sandown Park meeting. Bookmakers' telephones became hot with the panic; one bookmaker in Tattersall's offered the astounding odds of 10–1 and, surprisingly, didn't perish in a stampede. Earlier in the week Crepello had drifted from 5–4 to 6–4. Murless, somewhat testily, denied that Crepello had had an accident. His irritation was not hard to understand. Since Crepello's victory at Newmarket he had, successively, denied that Crepello was coughing, suffering from ringworm, or had developed 'a spot'. 'This latest rumour is fantastic, Murless said. 'Crepello could not have pleased me more in his Derby preparation since winning at Newmarket. This business is nonsense.'

In fact the Sandown Park episode was an interesting example of the potential for panic in an overheated betting fraternity. Any reasonable research would have established that Crepello had been moving smoothly and without mishap along the Limekilms gallop at Newmarket. Piggott, in tweed cap, sweater, and breeches, was delighted by the easy rhythm and the stirring of power as Crepello tracked his stable companion, Paper Moon, in a brisk five-furlong canter.

There was no hint of a cloud on the Warren Place horizon. There was a blue sky over the heath and by 10 am every day Crepello was back in his straw-lined, heavily guarded box. He was eating his food and sleeping like a top. But these facts, Murless's assurances, and a convincing explanation for the betting panic still left doubts among both bookies and the public. Crepello was 2–1 at the end of the day.

How did the panic start? Apparently a man who drew Crepello in a £20,000 sweepstake did some serious hedging. He approached some bookmakers seeking to lay £10,000 to £4,000 against Crepello. The bookmakers believed they sniffed a whole army of rats. The doubts persisted right up to the off. Two days before the race Captain Heath of the *News Chronicle* wrote:

> Crepello is the hot favourite for the Derby. Best price available about his chance is only 9–4 against. He won the Two Thousand Guineas at Newmarket, is free from any illness, and his owner and trainer express considerable optimism. He has been hailed generally as an outstanding horse likely to go on to win the Derby and the St Leger. But I beg to differ. I was not convinced after his success in the Two Thousand Guineas that Crepello is in the superhorse class. The challenge to him by Quorum – a high class handicapper but not really a horse of classic status – at the finish of the Guineas reduces the importance of Crepello's win, in my view. Quorum was nearly four lengths behind Crepello a furlong from the winning-post. He finished only half a length behind. I will not make a selection until I can be sure about the state of the going. But I will not be selecting Crepello.

Captain Heath's view was not a quirkish one. He was speaking for many who made their way to Epsom Downs on a cold, grey day in June 1957. The barbs aimed at Crepello were flicked away by Piggott, Murless and Sassoon, but they went more deeply into Jim Gunning. He felt like getting up on a soap-box at Epsom and telling the world about the quality of Crepello, 'my horse'.

Gunning, from Westmeath in Ireland, was Crepello's stable-lad. No one gets closer to a racehorse than a devoted stable-lad, and Gunning was with Crepello from the moment the colt arrived at Warren Place.

> I knew right from the start that I had been entrusted with a great racehorse. We saw straight away that he could really run, but he ate and rested well, too, and they are the signs of an intelligent horse. He hasn't lost me a wink of sleep. When Mr Murless came on stable inspections he invariably went to Crepello's box first. But I never had a twinge of concern. It was the same when we travelled. He never threw a mood or turned a hair. Because he loved work he gave you the feeling he was in a hurry to get to the racecourse.

But there was one question still unanswered in the minds of Murless and Piggott. How would the heavy-topped

Crepello handle Tattenham Corner? Would he maintain his rhythm at this decisive phase? They had hoped for an inkling of the answer on the morning of the race, but a shower had left the surface greasy and a trial run was cancelled. This, and another bad draw, were the snags, but they shrank beside the picture of Crepello during the preliminaries. He was as amiable as ever. He looked superb, for all the world a well-bred three-year-old enjoying his first party.

The draw meant that Piggott had to apply early speed. After a furlong the blaze of Crepello's head could be seen hovering between fifth and sixth place. Already Piggott had overcome a crisis. Crepello had left the start line less quickly than planned and for anxious seconds there seemed a danger that Piggott would have to spend much of the race seeking daylight. It was an idle fear. Piggott, it seemed could find daylight on a coal face.

1957 saw one of the roughest Derbies. When moderate leaders such as Chevastrid and Eudaeman lost momentum at Tattenham Corner accomplished jockeys such as Harry Carr (Doutelle), Bill Rickaby (Tempest) and champion Doug Smith (London Cry), had to swing wide to avoid disaster. Where was 21-year-old Lester Piggott? Just a width away from the corner rail; he had placed Crepello quite perfectly. Crepello was moving easily. Piggott could taste his third classic win. He had space and time and a feeling of utter serenity and this was amazing in the fury of Tattenham Corner. Piggott might have been operating a marionette show. He allowed Palor, a harmless outsider, a brief whirl, but when Tommy Burns took it up on Ballymoss (trained by Vincent O'Brien) it was time for more serious work. Piggott moved Crepello into the centre of the course and asked, rather as you might ask a small favour from an old friend, that Crepello move into a higher gear. The chestnut found lacerating speed. Doubts fell away from Crepello as Piggott eased him over the last few yards. He was a length and a half clear of Ballymoss.

Murless, watching from the Members' Enclosure, had been as still as his young jockey. Not a muscle twitched as Crepello overwhelmed Ballymoss. There was no inclination to gloat. There had never been that urge and nor would there be when Ballymoss went on to define the scale of Crepello's greatness on that cheerless Derby Day in 1957 with success at The Curragh, Doncaster, Sandown, back at Epsom, Royal Ascot, and, finally, Longchamp. By way of a reminder of his touch, he seven years later sired Royal Palace, which Murless trained to victory in the Two Thousand Guineas and the Derby. Ballymoss had run in a wide, brilliant circle.

Crepello's place in Derby history was assured as Piggott permitted himself two curt victory waves and a trace of a smile. Sir Victor Sassoon, victorious with Pinza four years earlier, was beside himself. He led Crepello into the unsaddling enclosure with a rare exuberance. When Piggott dismounted the happy owner rushed to pat him on the back, but he was frozen by a Piggott glare. The rules of racing are quite specific: a winning jockey must not have body contact before weighing in. Sassoon's outstretched hand hung limply and was withdrawn. Later, when he emerged from the jockeys' room, he was surrounded by admirers. He gave himself space, frowned and asked:

'What's there to it? I thought he was sure to win and he won. I never had a moment's anxiety.'

Although the race had often hinted at disaster, and ngotiating Tattenham Corner had made Hyde Park Corner at rush hour seem like a country crossroads, Piggott repeated his question:

'What's there to it?'

The Queen's jockey Harry Carr suggested an answer to the question. 'This was the worst race I have ever ridden in. The jockeys were not to blame. There were too many bad horses in the race and they kept dropping back and interfering with those who had a chance.'

The fact was that Piggott had put in a stunning performance and he knew it. The ghost of Charlie Smirke and Tulyar had finally galloped off into history. That Piggott had performed so well was confirmed in the after-race hubbub. Sir Gordon Richards, for whom Scobie Breasley had guided Pipe of Peace into third place, shook Piggott's hand and said, 'Your greatest race, something you can be really proud of.'

Rae Johnstone, winner in 1948, 1950 and 1956, simply said, 'Brilliant.' He shook his head and repeated, 'Brilliant.'

There was an echo – and it must have been the most gratifying piece of lip-reading for Piggott – from 'Smirkie'. The great Epsom specialist declared, 'That was terrific. Well done, son, you rode out of this world.' Piggott had brought in Crepello in 2 mins 35.4 secs, the fastest time since Smirke won on Mahmoud in 1936.

Crepello was, according to Noel Murless, 'the kindest horse I've ever known'. But he was also a meteor which flashed across the racing world. The Derby was his last race. Murless took him to Royal Ascot for the King George VI and Queen Elizabeth Stakes, and a vast throng prepared to pay tribute. They were frustrated and angry when Murless conferred with Piggott and Sassoon shortly before the race, and then announced that Crepello was being withdrawn.

There had been heavy rain and Murless fretted about the going, unreasonably so in the opinion of some critics. He felt that the soft going might expose Crepello to the risk of a pulled tendon. There were boos in Murless's ears but he didn't really hear them. He put Crepello into his box and went home. Neither he nor Crepello had anything to prove, and what were a few boos to set aside the well-being of his beloved horse? They could boo themselves into a frenzy but his horse would come first.

A month before the St Leger, Piggott worked Crepello at dawn. It was, as usual, an agreeable experience. There was all the old power and rhythm. There would be no water-skiing on St Leger day this year. Piggott exchanged a few words with the stable-lad Gunning and then Murless before driving away from Warren Place. He was in good spirits. Another classic danced before him.

That evening Murless made his tour of inspection and, as always, went first to Crepello's box. Murless ran his hands along Crepello's forelegs and suddenly caught his breath. He felt heat in the tendon which runs from knee to fetlock. He had withdrawn Crepello from Ascot precisely because of this fear. The fears which had never been far from Murless's thoughts throughout Crepello's career were confirmed the following morning when the vet called at Warren Place. Crepello was out of the St Leger. And out of racing: he had gone lame.

Piggott was very upset.

> I didn't detect any unsoundness in his movement. It's a tragedy. I'm sure that but for those legs he would have been the first horse since Bahram in 1935 to win the Triple Crown. He was absolutely right in the Two Thousand Guineas and the Derby and won both races comfortably. He beat Ballymoss comfortably in the Derby and I'm sure he would have done so again in the Leger.

Years later Piggott still insisted, 'I never really did anything. Crepello won by himself. He was a truly great horse, kind to everyone and prepared to do his best whenever he was asked.' Crepello may have missed the Leger, never travelled to the green beauty of Longchamp, but he left no doubts in the minds of Noel Murless and Lester Piggott. Crepello's greatest achievement was beyond the racecourse. He did something which was too demanding for most humans – he brought a smile to the face of Lester Piggott. He brought the best out of him, both as a jockey and as a man.

8 A Present for the Queen

The young Queen of England, wearing a blue silk dress, stood in the passage beside the weighing-room at Epsom. Her face showed a trace of that tension known to anyone who has ever had to wait and wonder about the result of a photo finish. The Duke of Edinburgh expressed optimism. The Queen gave a thin smile. Outside, a quarter of a million of her subjects were hushed. At last there was a loudspeaker announcement, swiftly lost in a great roll of patriotic thunder. Judge John Hancock had announced that the Queen's Carrozza had won the 1957 Oaks. The margin of the victory was defined, officially, as nine inches! It could scarcely have been finer, nor could the scale of the winning jockey's achievement have been greater. Lester Piggott, two days after completing the Two Thousand Guineas and Derby double on Crepello, had added the Oaks to his belt. The treble feat had last been performed sixty-two years earlier by Fred Archer. It seemed that Piggott was galloping in the very hoofprints of his great and tragic hero. Like Archer, he fought a relentless battle against the scales, his nature seemed irredeemably drawn to melancholy, and some of his riding left professional observers stunned by its power, splendour and extraordinary timing.

If there is anything in racing that can be described as a 'sure thing' – and those who know the game best insist there isn't – it is that one day Piggott will be summoned to Buckingham Palace and to become Sir Lester. It seems equally certain that when the Queen performs the ceremony her thoughts will travel back to that day at Epsom when she first knew the thrill of owning a classic winner. Her joy that afternoon radiated across the downs. The victory had been so dramatic, so unexpected, so much the product of one man's astonishing will.

In the early years of the Queen's reign the energies of many great sportsmen and adventureers were dramatically released. Everest had fallen to Hillary and Tensing as a coronation celebration. Cricket had the elusive genius of Graveney, the formidable technique of May and Cowdrey and the fast bowlers, Trueman, Statham and Tyson, were challenging Australian supremacy. On the football field Manchester United were performing extraordinary deeds. In the Welsh valleys there was Dai Dower, the charming flyweight with twinkling feet and a mop of black curly hair. They have all retired now, of course; only Piggott remains lean, apparently ageless and honed for action. Since his epic ride on Carrozza the demon of competition has remained rampant. Back in the fifties people spoke hopefully of a new Elizabethan age, when Englishmen would be filled with optimism and adventure. It was a brief notion, largely destroyed by the cynicism which greeted the Suez disaster, but while it lasted it could be said that the young Lester Piggott embodied some of the qualities which epitomize golden ages. There was nothing more acceptable than the prize Piggott presented to the Queen that day at Epsom; it was an unexpected victory, the achievement of which lent weight to Keith Piggott's theory that his son was then exploring the extent of his talent.

Piggott senior, who had watched over his son's career zealously right back from his first pony ride across the yard at Lambourn, suggests that Piggott is perfect because he was absolutely untouched by fear. He would never be physically afraid. Indeed, he has said that if he ever felt a hint of fear he would immediately retire. If so, Piggott might have considered retirement at Epsom in 1977 when the Oaks candidate Durtal, sweating heavily, slipped her saddle and dragged Piggott towards the paddock rails. The crowd screamed at the prospect of a sickening collision, but a stirrup-leather broke and Piggott rolled clear. The next afternoon he was riding, as hard as ever, at Chantilly. It was fear of implications that Keith Piggott was talking about; fear that the cumulative effect of suspensions and ill-informed criticism would weaken his faith in all-out style, and that the ignorance of stewards would deny him victories brilliantly drawn from his great reservoir of nerve and courage.

At the time of Crepello and Carrozza Piggott was involved in a stupendous gallop towards the sixties. It was, as Keith Piggott suggests, as though Piggott's youthful intensity was burning out in a glorious, crackling conflagration all those who couldn't ride with the same fearless abandon. He would become smarter; his knowledge of horses and pace would become more profound, his eye for opportunity might sharpen. But there was a strong feeling among the experts at Epsom on the afternoon of the 1957 Oaks that Lester Piggott would never ride a better race than this one he had put in for his Queen.

Today Sir Noel Murless, who trained Carrozza and who has seen so much of Piggott from many different angles, remains emphatic about that last point. After the race Murless seemed to be numb with pleasure and pride and a hint of wonderment.

> I knew then that this brilliant jockey could never surpass his riding of Carrozza. There just couldn't be anything better. He might be able to reproduce a similar performance. But never exceed it. Oh no, I knew certainly that this was something quite out of the ordinary.

The Queen had a more fancied runner in the 1957 Oaks, Mulberry Harbour, ridden by the royal jockey Harry Carr and trained by Captain Boyd Rochfort. However, Mulberry Harbour's challenge faded at Tattenham Corner. Piggott, once again, had negotiated Epsom perfectly. Carrozza had been kept in touch, given good ground, but a hundred yards from the post she seemed to be going the same way as Mulberry Harbour. She looked as though her last reserves had been tapped, but might fight out a place. The Irish filly Silken Glider, ridden by Jimmy Eddery, appeared much the stronger. Piggott had moved beautifully along the rails and pushed Carrozza's nose into a fractional lead, but it was apparently no more than the last desperate gesture of a young man fiercely prejudiced against the idea of conceding defeat. The consensus in the great stand was that the order would be Silken Glider, Rose Royale II, the favourite, and Carrozza third.

Piggott simply refused to accept it. He brought the whip down on Carrozza. In the trade it is euphemistically called a 'reminder'. It is really more a call to dramatic action, an exhortation to stride through the closing grip of fatigue. Piggott sat still, perfectly still, and the miracle happened: Carrozza rallied. There was a great swell of sound on the downs. A beaten horse was suddenly producing something more. Nothing warms the blood of a race crowd as much as the sight of gameness along the straight. The aristocrats, Nijinsky, Mill Reef and Sir Ivor are applauded for their intelligence and beauty. Carrozza was applauded straight from the heart. She was, after all, the Queen's horse.

Silken Glider and Carrozza were together at the front, but they were not in stride. As each filly made her stride forward the lead was reversed, and remained the same for a hundred yards to the post. First Silken Glider, then Carrozza inched ahead, Normally sober observers roared. The Queen craned forward, caught her breath. She has always loved horses and been deeply thrilled by the drama and the colour of the turf. Everyone agreed that it was probably the finest finish they would ever see. Few could agree, though, on the winner.

The wait for the photographic verdict seemed interminable. The royal party were poised to welcome Piggott and Carrozza, but there was no way of knowing whether it would be in glory or simply the gratitude that goes out to those who have done a great service. In the background there were loyal cries that Piggott had done it. A large Irishman bravely offered the conclusion that Jimmy Eddery had got there.

Piggott patted the brave filly. It was partly to soothe, partly to salute. And he waited, aloof, his face devoid of any emotion, a blank sheet upon which strain and wasting had not yet scratched their marks. He nodded when the verdict came – and patted Carrozza once more. Carrozza's margin had been a fraction of a stride! It was the first royal classic win at Epsom for forty-eight years.

The Queen, radiant if slightly shy, led Carrozza into the winners' enclosure. It was a difficult manoeuvre. The crowd, a bobbing press of fine hats, roared and Carrozza seemed unnerved. Piggott whispered to the filly and the Queen took a firm grip on the leading rein. Carrozza was safe, the royal party went happily away to champagne, and Lester Piggott had to lip-read his way through another tide of congratulations. Again he protested at the fuss. Was he not simply doing his job? Did draughtsmen and engineers and bricklayers not have days which were better than others? This time, though, he did admit to Sir Gordon Richards that it was probably his best professional performance. The background tumult was of superlatives. Piggott relentlessly talked only of professional work. Sir Gordon had been the first to seize Piggott's hand after the Crepello triumph. Again, he was one of the first to congratulate the young pretender to his own abdicated crown, but this time he did it with a new conviction, a new gravity.

Sir Gordon now knew he was being succeeded by a genius.

By resisting the temptation to eat and by depriving himself of all the other good things in life that a young man wants Lester Piggott has shown the most amazing strength of character. The secret of Lester Piggott is confidence in his own genius. For he is a genius as Steve Donoghue was before. From the very beginning he always had known instinctively what to do – and when to do it. Take Epsom, the trickiest course of them all. Lester never worries about the bends or the crowding or the changing ground or what the other jockeys are doing – or might be planning to do. Like Steve, he gets into exactly the right position – about fourth or fifth – and then at the psychological moment he goes. That was how he won the Oaks on Carrozza.

I agreed with him that this was the best race I have ever seen him ride. Everyone must agree with that, surely. Everything about his performance was right. He rode the perfect race and when it seemed that it was not enough, well, right away he produced something more. There is no rational explanation of how he got Carrozza home. We come back to the word genius – a man's ability to communicate something to a horse. Just think of it! Think of his age. He was riding for the Queen – and it was the Oaks. Think of the pressure that would put on any man, of any age or experience. But it made no difference to Lester, of course. He behaved just as if it was a selling race and precisely at the right moment, before the other jockeys knew what was happening, he went.

Believe me, Lester Piggott stole that race. A lot of nonsense has been talked and written about Lester, his behaviour on and off a horse. For example, that story of him saying to me 'move over grandpa' during a race was quite untrue. Of course he would stand up for himself if necessary, but I always found him very respectful and well mannered. None of the rough riding was a deliberate effort to be dangerous or unfair. It was all part and parcel of his genius. He just knew that he had to be in a certain place at a certain moment in order to win.

It is extraordinary that this eulogy was delivered not by some adoring devotee of a great figure retiring at the end of a long, rich lifetime but by one of the finest jockeys who ever lifted himself into a saddle – and about a mere boy, an aloof, unfathomable kid, who had three years earlier brusquely rejected the offer of a job! In Richards's generous way he was explaining some of the extraordinary impact Piggott had already made. Even if some mishap had overtaken Lester Piggott in the autumn of 1957, if his will to make the weights had snapped or his thirst for riding winners had suddenly been slaked, there is no question that his place in racing history would not have been secure. He had the sort of year which has eluded so many fine jockeys. It was the year when he implicitly announced, beyond all doubt, that he was a master rider.

Noel Murless knew that he had lost nothing in the exchange of Richards for Piggott except, possibly, the former's edge in the sprints. Murless still reveres Sir Gordon Richards, both as a jockey and as a man, but in 1957 he was able to say:

In a big race over a long distance, Piggott is as good as Gordon was. And Lester is improving each year. He gets a little tougher, a little shrewder. His eyes are open all the time. He doesn't miss a thing. I do not have to lecture Piggott about the job, the special nature of a particular race. I may remind him of a horse's special characteristics, but when you employ a QC you do not presume to tell him how to go about his job. A QC has years of experience and learning behind him. Well, so does young Piggott. He knows his profession. He could not be more dedicated.

But, to return to the question posed in newspapers seven years earlier, at what cost did Piggott acquire this excellence? Was his life turning into a programme of endeavour which excluded from his life the simple but important joys of youth? Sir Gordon's eulogy hints at the thought of an austere young man locked into an endless cycle of racing.

Susan Goswell did more than suggest this, she stated it as a fact. Susan Goswell was the daughter of a jockey, and became Lester Piggott's first girlfriend. Like him, she had grown up with horses. She was a Lambourn girl. Her father had been badly injured, and she knew more of the other side of racing, the broken dreams, the unfulfilled yearnings. She and Piggott were friends for a long time.

Parties, dances, special affairs in the district, we were there. We had so much fun in those days. He used to enjoy himself. But since he became so busy, so famous, I don't see very much of him. Lester seems to have no time at all to enjoy life. It all seems so serious and grim. I wonder if it is worth it, just for money?

'Just for money'! You might as well say that Michaelangelo smashed his chisel into the knee of his statue of Moses because of pressure from his bank manager. But it is certainly true that by the standards of the late fifties Lester Piggott was fabulously rich. In 1959 Murless shattered the prize-winning record with £145,727 and Piggott's share of that was a minimum £10,000. A grateful Sir Victor Sassoon presented him with a Lincoln Continental. It was promptly sold, converted into crisp banknotes. Sir Victor talked about a trust fund for his wonder jockey, and in France, trainers bruised themselves in the crush to sign him for special rides. By 1959 Piggott's earnings were estimated at £30,000 a year. At that time Bobby Charlton, Johnny Haynes and Sir Stanley Matthews were earning around £20 a week.

To say that it was pound notes Lester Piggott saw before his eyes in the last hundred yards of the 1957 Oaks seems a nonsense to me. A master of the stock exchange who can make fortunes in New York, Zurich and London in a matter of minutes is not successful because he loves money. What he loves is the hunch that pays off, the speed of the decisions, the marvellous computer buzz of his own brain. It is a statement about himself. Piggott has been dispassionate about many of his horses, for the same reason, one suspects, that the financial wizard does not take bundles of banknotes home in order to fondle and admire them. Horses have been Piggott's means of making a statement about himself.

One also suspects that money has been for Piggott merely a measurement of his success. If this was not so he would have retired long ago. His knowledge of the world's stock exchanges is encyclopaedic. He could have installed a telex in his Newmarket home and dabbled in the markets, easily handling the shifts and stresses of the money markets, and the odds are that he would have augmented his personal fortune. But he would have ceased to be the world's best jockey, ceased to have that special knowledge that on your day you are untouchable. Susan Goswell, like so many people, didn't understand that about Lester Piggott.

9 An Appetite for Winning

Lester Piggott's old friend and great rival Jimmy Lindley explained to me the psychology of wasting. It is not something you dip into, like a cold shower, or flirt with, like the morning jog. It is perpetual. It becomes part of you; let go, and you're lost. It is essential to understand this endless tyranny in which big brother is a set of scales before beginning to get close to the inner nature of Lester Piggott.

Wasting helped kill Fred Archer. It has been the shadow over so many sportsmen who had all the talent in the world but who had nothing to spare in the crucial matter of will-power. Their talent dribbled to nothing in the steam bath; their ambitions were eaten away by the gnawing pain in their stomachs. For every Ernest Hemingway, who claimed that when he growled with hunger he could best appreciate the line and the depth of the great paintings in the Louvre, there are ten jockeys who will tell you that, in the end, there is not a trophy or a purse which adequately compensates for living in hell. Wasting is miserable because it is unnatural; it is a decision of the brain inflicted on the body, and the body kicks and snarls, and never lets the mind forget what it is doing. According to Jimmy Lindley, wasting is always going to be hard.

> It is always going to demand great discipline, great dedication. But the key to it, how well you can tackle it, is what sort of success you get along the way. You sweat blood and make the weight and ride a winner and all the pain and the misery seems worthwhile; you finish up on a loser and you are at rockbottom. I would put it

this way: with glory you can live on an egg, with failure you need a minimum of five pounds of steak.

Lindley grew up in the game with Piggott. He was a fine jockey in his own right; strong, brave as they come, sharp-witted in the matter of drawing up shrewd tactics. More than once he delivered a hurtful *coup de grâce* to the maestro. But he is the first to admit that even when they were boys you could draw a line between the two. On Lindley's side there was a great love of horses and racing, a fascination and a pleasure. On Piggott's side there was something more, stemming from his ferocious ambition. It was a quality that seemed to come from another world, some inner thrust which rode over the merest hint that getting first past the post wasn't life's only horizon. Lindley recognized early in their relationship that Piggott could indeed live on glory and an egg. He could make a vast, richly-flavoured omelette of it.

The thing about Lester, even now, is that you could ring him on Boxing Day and ask him, 'Can you make 8 st 10 lb for a good thing at Santa Anita?' and you can be sure what the answer will be. He would be there, strong, under control. I've gone out on a Saturday night 8 st 4 lb, and woken up on Sunday morning at 9 st 4 lb. I cannot imagine Lester ever having given himself that much to do. It's just not in the way he thinks. His mother gave him a good start. When I visited the family in Lambourn I noticed how Mrs Piggott would insist that Lester have a black coffee or a piece of melon. I also noticed that, unlike some of us, he would always take a bite or two during the day. Some of us would starve through the day, stomachs growling, feel weak as kittens at night and then just blow out.

There was never anything so erratic with Lester. He was determined to stay on top of it. It was as though he knew it would be one of the most important aspects of his life so he decided to come to terms with it early, and he would never let go. I don't think it really hurt him as it hurts me and maybe people like Harry Carr and Charlie Smirke. Of course it was incredible dedication. But when we come back to my first point that Lester has always been able to justify his sacrifices in his own mind. The girl who worries about her figure suffers and finds it all a terrible strain. But really the only thing at stake for her, at least in the short term, is her vanity. For Lester it is everything. The whole tone of his life is conditioned by how he fares professionally. He knows what he has to do and he knows what the rewards will be if he does it.

And such rewards. Harry Carr, the royal jockey, might offer the opinion that young Piggott was slowly killing himself, drying himself out to a freakish degree, but the young man would never want for incentive while Murless went about producing superhorses. Murless could deliver from under any pressure, any burden of expectation. Certainly, after the brilliance of Crepello and the bravery of Carrozza, the temptation was to say to him, what do you have for your next trick, how do you propose to follow those two?

Murless was waiting for the question, happily enough. He produced a grey filly, Petite Etoile, who would be known variously as the 'silver wonder', 'the super filly' and even the 'filly of the century'. More soberly, she was described as the best filly since Pretty Polly enlivened the first years of this century. She was a stunner, proud and pert, and named for the small pink star at the end of her pretty nose. But though she would clearly adorn Warren Place the first reaction to her at Newmarket was not one of overwhelming confidence. When The Aly Khan suggested that he might send Petite Etoile, a daughter of Petition, to England his principal trainer, Alec Head, did not demur. She looked nice enough, but Head was awash with expensive yearlings at Chantilly and it seemed to him that although Petite Etoile might well prosper he would probably survive in her absence. Alec Head was to win many more great victories; enough, in fact, to obliterate the most drastic of mistakes. But it would nonetheless be heartless to mention the name of Petite Etoile in the presence of Alec Head; it is an old but still raw wound. Lester Piggott was more fortunate. He, like St Peter, had three chances to get it right and, at the third invitation, he said yes, he would ride Petite Etoile.

His first rejection came before the Free Handicap, George Moore taking the ride, successfully. On the second occasion it was the Thousand Guineas and Doug Smith underlined the merit of Petite Etoile. By the Oaks Piggott had long joined the converted and his only comfort, and that of Alec Head's was that Murless had not been immediately convinced when the filly arrived from France. It took some time before Murless became confident about her.

We had her as a yearling and we knew she was going to be an outstanding individual and certain to race. She came from a fast family and always showed plenty of speed – but I didn't really think she would have the staying power. It was at Goodwood that I first realized she had the stamina too and after talking to Prince Aly we decided to give her a chance in the Free Handicap. Soon I could say I had never seen a horse quite like her. A super horse is like a super human being. It has to have the same qualities. It has to have the physical capabilities and then it has to have that something extra. It has to have that will to win.

Piggott's resistance to Petite Etoile had been based entirely on the question of stamina. Undoubtedly she was a beauty, and highly aware of her own charms. She was the queen of Warren Place's Garden Yard and her beauty was enhanced by the lilac and laburnum in her corner of the great stables.

Murless adored her, relented at her first nuzzle for one of the sugar lumps he kept in the pockets of his tweed jacket. Murless is the least effusive of men but he could scarcely contain himself on the topic of his grey filly.

Hers is a woman's face and a woman's character. She has a very nice, well-bred nature but if anything upsets her, well then, all hell breaks loose. She knows she's good. She doesn't stand for any other horses eating near her – she insists that they stay at a respectful distance. She is the most intelligent animal I have ever known. She misses nothing. She instantly recognizes me a hundred yards away and demands her present of sugar. She also has a wonderful sense of humour. Sometimes in the box I will pick up a stick and raise it to her in fun and she immediately picks up her leg at me. Any owner or trainer would be very, very exceptionally lucky to get one the likes of her just once in a lifetime.

Beyond the beauty, the engaging personality, the acceptable arrogance there was the most exciting quality of all in a racehorse: she had a turn of foot which was simply dazzling. With one imperceptible change of gear Petite Etoile flew. It is a mixture of rhythm, wind, build, leg and some sublime natural mystery. She was to beat Derby-winner Parthia in the first of her two Coronation Cup triumphs. Piggott brought her smoothly to the Oaks finishing post, pressing the throttle late but with such unanswerable power that it seemed as though Cantelo (ridden by Eddie Hide) and Rose of Medina (Ephie Smith) had turned to stone. Until beaten by Sir Winston Churchill's High Hat, in an Ascot race designed as a memorial to her owner, Petite Etoile was bathed in awe and affection. Piggott had never been so closely examined by critics and public. Some voices, including the much respected one of Roger Mortimer, claimed that Piggott's handling of Petite Etoile was in fact obscuring the full range of her talent. It was suggested that Piggott's habit of releasing her only at the last moment was denying her the chance to prove the scale of her greatness. The theory was that if Piggott released her earlier she would simply annihilate her opposition. Piggott was unimpressed with the argument. Of course, he said, Petite Etoile was marvellous, so wonderfully fast; but he insisted her talent had to be carefully marshalled. It was an extraordinary talent but such ability has to be tended like a rare bloom. Only a fool would leave it unprotected. You would not abuse a talent of this quality, he argued. But he admitted that he should have beaten Jimmy Lindley and Aggressor at Royal Ascot.

Petite Etoile was always great fun to ride. She was intelligent and a good looker. Fillies, as we all know, can be deceptive. You sometimes find one who doesn't look all that much but will run until she drops. Petite Etoile did not really stay, but she had this incredible burst of speed. The ability to paralyse anything in a burst of speed over a hundred yards can make both a horse and a jockey look the best in the world. The crowds love this sort of thing, holding a position behind the leaders and then going like the wind. We were beaten by Jimmy Lindley on Aggressor and I should have won. I took what I thought was the best way on the outside because there was a wall of horses in front of the filly and Aggressor. At that moment the horses in front of us split up and Jimmy was able to go through on the inside. I had to go a little before time and with Aggressor away Petite Etoile could not produce her speed for long enough. We were dead before we got near the post.

It is clear that Piggott's fine measuring of Petite Etoile's resources did give Murless and The Aly Khan's racing manager, Major Cyril Hall, some painful twinges. On the morning of the Champion Stakes at Newmarket both men appealed to him.

Piggott, head cocked quizzically, heard Murless say, 'Lester, let us go easy on anxiety today, please.' Murless is by nature a practical man; what he was asking for was something other than practicality. He was breaking his own rule, which insisted that if you hire a QC you don't stand up yourself until it is absolutely necessary. Even by his own standards of refrigerated nerve, Piggott cut the Champion Stakes very fine. In the final furlong it seemed that Piggott was coolly aiming to send Petite Etoile through a slender gap between her rivals Barclay and Javelot. Garnie Bougoure, Barclay's rider, was startled more than he should have been by the dawning awareness of what Piggott was about to do. But he kept his nerve and, quite legally, closed off the daylight between himself and Javelot, who was ridden by Freddy Palmer. Piggott never faltered. He drove for the rails, despite the fact that Javelot appeared to block any progress other than ground to air work, which so far Piggott had not attempted. Some of the crowd gasped. Some, those whose money was riding with Piggott, groaned. It seemed that Piggott had ridden himself into the blindest of alleys. He could only ride through Javelot, which was physically difficult and legally questionable, certainly with a record like his. Then something happened. Palmer's efforts to maintain Javelot's rhythm suddenly faltered, Javelot's hindquarters swung outwards and there on the rail was just a glimmer of light. Piggott hurled Petite Etoile at the gap and beneath him there was that magical stirring, that sudden speed which carries horse-racing into a new level of experience.

Petite Etoile and Piggott came home by half a length. It was a heist so daring some onlookers rubbed their eyes. Others simply shrugged their shoulders and said, 'Well, of course, it's Piggott.'

Later Freddy Palmer asked a question to which he knew there really was no answer! 'How could Lester Piggott have done such a thing? It doesn't seem possible.' He might have been asking why the sun came up each morning. Murless and Major Hall, relief and irritation warring in their brains, were told brusquely by Piggott, 'I could still have run round the other side and won.'

Piggott's style, his imagination and his daring, merely astonished Freddy Palmer. But one French jockey was so enraged by it he spent most of the 1959 French Oaks using his whip on Piggott. After the race the Frenchman went to the Chantilly stewards and reported his action. He said he was owning up in case there were any complaints. Piggott, he said, had turned Epsom into a purgatory for French jockeys. Piggott didn't complain. In the week following his Epsom Oaks triumph he was suspended by the Nottingham stewards for rough riding. These complaints and suspensions had become irritations, but he dealt with them as if swatting flies. He knew, beyond doubt, that his career could scarcely be set on firmer ground. He was in demand on the Continent. He had made his American début. Sir Victor Sassoon had come along with Crepello, the Queen with Carrozza, and the Aly Khan with Petite Etoile. The Aly Khan was nearing the end of his life, and his grey filly and her brilliant young rider had brought a thrilling, colourful climax to his racing days. In August 1959 he flew to York and watched the partnership gather up the Yorkshire Oaks. The race had that fine quality which gives the turf its hold over the imagination of many fabulously wealthy men. The sight of Piggott unleashing Petite Etoile left the Prince elated. He congratulated Murless and Piggott and flew back to France. 'I bred Petite Etoile, you know,' he said with pride, 'and she's the best filly I've ever seen.' It was something for a man to be able to say. He warmed himself on the thought as his private aeroplane skipped the channel.

It was Sir Victor Sassoon's turn to bring something to Warren Place. This time his offering was St Paddy. For Sir Victor, too, it was to be his last big romance with the turf. He bred St Paddy. The colt could trace his family tree back to the legendary Pretty Polly, though first impressions hinted that the best genes had not made a bee-line down the decades in search of St Paddy.

He was a late developer and was raced only twice as a two-year-old. He was unplaced in his first race and though he had five lengths to spare in his second, Ascot's Royal Lodge Stakes, the opposition was weak. He had a touch of class, although you could neither quantify it nor suggest how far it would take him. Certainly it wouldn't take him to a triumphant Two Thousand Guineas. It was his first race as a three-year-old and though he encouraged optimism over the first six furlongs, running smoothly and looking well, his lack of racecourse work began to show when he was challenged. Warren Place and racing remained unimpressed by St Paddy. If Murless had felt a shaft of certainty when he watched Crepello and Petite Etoile strike their lovely, surging rhythm, he found himself hoping rather than believing in St Paddy. Piggott increased Murless's hopes when he brought him in comfortably for the Dante Stakes at York, but again the field was adjudged poor. Piggott gave a good report to Murless. However, the evidence remained slender; there had been no stretching, no real examination.

St Paddy would have to explain himself at Epsom. He had flickered with promise, shown snatches of genius power. He suffered in comparison with Crepello and Petite Etoile, and there were rumblings from the French about Angers. The French claimed he was their best thing for years. He had been the dominant French two-year-old and had flown to victory in the Prix Hocquart, which is run over the Derby distance. Ireland's Die Hard, son of Never Say Die, was much fancied at 9–2 and St Paddy's chances were aligned with those of the Irish contenders, Kythnos, Irish Two Thousand Guineas winner and Tulyartos. These three were offered at 7–1.

St Paddy won the Derby all right. Piggott's antennae were in perfect working order. He studied every patch of good ground, measured the opposition, sounded out St Paddy, and then made the big move so smoothly and suddenly that his rivals were simply floored. The early pace was so sedate that Die Hard, not one of life's true workers, was able to make the running, and after slipping back into the pack going down into Tattenham Corner he reappeared at the front as the field swung into the straight. Auroy and Marengo presented themselves at Die Hard's hindquarters, but no sooner had they done so than Piggott and St Paddy were thrusting through. Scobie Breasley, baulked at Tattenham Corner, coaxed Paddy Prendergast's colt Alcaeus into second place, just ahead of his stable companion Kythnos.

It was a neat defeat of the doubters of St Paddy, but where was the euphoria as Piggott the wonder-boy brought to the unsaddling enclosure his third Derby winner in six years? St Paddy seemed fated to live away from the bright glow of untarnished glory. Piggott, Murless, and Sassoon might claim that their colt was a good, comfortable Derby winner; indeed, Piggott today claims it as his easiest Derby win.

But the thousands of people who filed away from Epsom were not thinking of the young jockey and the colt who had saved the best running of his life for the biggest day in English racing; they were thinking of Angers, the French colt who was being put down just as Piggott was sliding from St Paddy's saddle. The equine gods had looked sourly on the 1960 Derby. The Irish colt Exchange Student had broken a leg and been put down during a trial run on the eve of the race. Sir Winston Churchill's fancied contender Vienna had been 'pricked' by the blacksmith on the morning of the race and had been withdrawn. The Angers tragedy came on the approach to Tattenham Corner. French jockey Gerard Thiboeuf had been told by his trainer, Gerald Bridgland, an Englishman who worked in Chantilly, to lay back and do his work in the straight. After the race Thiboeuf picked at his meal in a French restaurant in London and said, 'There was no weakness in Angers. No one touched us. I think we were in the main group of horses and I was quite happy. We were going well. Then suddenly we fell.'

For the spectators on the rails a terrible chill entered an afternoon of gaiety and excitement. They saw unfolding before their eyes the sort of tragedy and pain which all racing men, especially those charging into Tattenham Corner, know is always just a stride away. A spectator gave this graphic description of the end of a fine racehorse:

The horses came round in a tight bunch. Suddenly Angers stumbled and seemed to go forward on his knees. The jockey was thrown off. A man ran out of the crowd and grabbed Angers's head. The horse stood there for a moment after picking himself up and a policeman took his bridle. The starter's car arrived and the jockey was taken into it. Then the vet's car came up. The horse was standing still with his left foreleg raised. Twice he tried to put weight on the broken leg and each time he jumped and tried to tug himself away. The policeman tried to calm him and then the vet came forward with the humane killer. . . .

Angers's owner, eighty-year-old Mrs Ralph Strassburger, the wife of an American newspaper tycoon, was ignorant of her colt's fate for several minutes. Anxiously, she asked what had happened. Had Angers finished? Had there been an accident? She asked Peter O'Sullevan to find out. 'Please,' she said, 'he is such a wonderful horse.'

When O'Sullevan returned with the bleak news her eyes filled with tears and she said, 'I suppose we must expect these tragedies in racing.'

St Paddy would have to wait for the glory, and when he did reappear at Goodwood the cloud of tragedy at Epsom was replaced by the harsh light of humiliation. Kipling, whose biggest day had been victory in the 'dockers' Derby' (the Irwell Stakes) at Manchester, outlasted St Paddy in the final furlong, winning by half a length. Murless was bruised but not despairing. He worked hard, insisted that he would restore St Paddy to proper status, and there was encouragement when St Paddy carried away the Voltigeur Stakes at York.

St Paddy was favourite for the St Leger and he ran like a favourite. Piggott had to keep him on the bit. Murless had never won the St Leger before, and it was strange to think that this colt, previously weighed down by the faintest of praise, should run superbly on Derby Day and St Leger day.

St Paddy started his four-year-old career with a glorious surge. Then he wavered. He finished downbeat, being thoroughly defeated in the Champion Stakes. Right from the start he had been a mass of contradictions. He would not, even at this early stage, enter the first rank of horses ridden by Lester Piggott. Yet he had won the Derby and the Leger, and £97,000 in prize money.

10 The Right Kind of Partner

If 1960 was the year of St Paddy it was also, more crucially for Lester Piggott, the year of Susan, his bride. On a February day of low cloud and drizzle the couple were married at St Mark's Church, North Audley Street, London W1.

Piggott was spruce, hair slicked and shining. He wore a blue-striped suit with built-up shoulders and raised trouser seams. Onlookers observed that they had seen him looking far more relaxed waiting for the verdict of a big race photograph. Susan, daughter of trainer Sam Armstrong, wore beige. She was twenty, Piggott was twenty-four. There were thirty-eight guests, most of them ruddy-faced from the country air.

When the party moved down the road to Brown's Hotel they found a hundred telegrams. If you had gathered the senders together and deported them the British turf would have collapsed. There was champagne and smoked salmon and attentive waiters, but it was not an uproarious affair. The Piggotts are not that kind of people, nor are the Armstrongs. They are racing people, but, above all, horse and country people. A country church would really have been more suitable, but it was decided that a Newmarket wedding would have meant a town besieged.

Susan Armstrong, 5 ft 1 in tall, was trim and attractive, crisp and direct. Piggott had been drawn to her looks and her manner, and there had never been any awkwardness because he sensed, straight away, that they had much in common. Susan rode with panache and skill and great courage. She had won, like Piggott's mother, the Newmarket

Ladies Plate. If Lester Piggott, when faced with the task of choosing a wife, had fed his needs into a computer and the whole application had been scientifically programmed, the result would have been Susan Armstrong.

Unlike Susan Goswell of Lambourn, Susan Armstrong of Newmarket understood Lester Piggott right from the start. There were no great mysteries or painful adjustments. She understood implicitly that her husband's life would be entwined with horses and their seasons. A conventional life buoyed up by the comforting props of domesticity would have been as alien to her as it would to her partner. She knew that she would not be putting out the great Piggott's slippers at the same time each evening; she was marrying a superstar with all the bizarre intrusions which that status brought. It was feasible to her because, as she would privately admit, Lester Piggott's life was exactly the one she would have chosen had she been a man. She, too, was fascinated by the rhythms of horse-racing, the subtle forces of breeding, the uncertainties which would always exist until the animal was past the post.

Sam Armstrong lost more than a daughter in exchange for a son-in-law already galloping into the foothills of legend. He lost a skilled trainer of horses, a girl who could be left in charge of his St Gatien stables without causing the remotest twinge of concern. Piggott acquired rather more than a devoted wife and mother of their two daughters, a briskly-efficient secretary and, eventually, business manager; he found a fierce protector, a shield against an inquisitive world. Anyone who has ever attempted to invade the time of Lester Piggott will know about the effectiveness of the shield. She does for Piggott roughly what the Swiss Guards do for the Pope.

John Morgan, former sports editor of the *Daily Express* who knew the Piggotts first professionally, then personally, describes Lester Piggott's life at home.

There are some great misconceptions about Lester and his life. One of them is that he is a cheerless character. You only have to be in the Piggott home for a few hours to realize that it is a place of great warmth and animation and humour. Lester can unwind beautifully and Susan never seems to tire of acting as a kind of screen, a protector. Their home can be unbelievable on a Sunday morning.

The phone becomes red-hot. Trainers and owners, writers and punters, all kinds of people are trying to snatch a few words with Lester. Susan weeds them out. She makes his life work smoothly. When you think about it, it's a hell of a job and the fact is that she has always been on top of it. She's very feminine, of course, but you get a little distracted from that because she is so strong, so capable and business-like. It was interesting that when she had a bad fall from a horse, and her face was a mess for a while, she just retreated into her shell. She refused to show herself, wouldn't go to the door. You thought, good heavens, she is affected by female vanity.

Another strong-minded lady, Jean Rook, met her at Royal Ascot and later observed, 'Mrs Piggott is stirrup-high, jockey slim, and without binoculars you could miss her. She is reputed to be as taciturn as Lester, and some people say they communicate by tic-tac.' Susan Piggott's response is characteristically direct.

That's rubbish and all part of Lester's image. For a start, I have some beautiful pictures of him smiling. In fact we have photographs all over the house. There isn't space for any more. Where do people get the idea that Lester is an untalkative misery? He is extremely amusing and very dry. What I like best about him – and there are so many things I like about him it is hard to pick one out – is his sense of humour, believe it or not. He will have you in stitches on the way home, describing a race from his point of view. He will tell me exactly how it went, every bump, every gap – and the precise moment he knew he would win or lose. I admit we talk horses a lot but it's only natural. My father was a trainer and I was born to it. It doesn't bore me. I must say I think it could be terrible if you were married to a jockey and you didn't understand the job and the complete dedication. Lester is totally dedicated.

She recognized that Piggott had a status which could carry him far beyond the superstar category. He could, given his momentum at the start of the sixties, become a one-man industry. That being so, her wedding-gift to her husband was inspired. She gave him a desk. But after setting up their first home at Florizel, just off Newmarket High Street, she moved into that desk herself, becoming an astute business manager for her husband. Few young brides could have set up home more confident in the knowledge that they had attached themselves to a born winner.

Within four months of their honeymoon in Nice he would bring home St Paddy, his third Derby win. In the autumn he would be crowned champion and when this happened few people doubted that it was the opening statement in a long speech establishing superiority. It seemed that Piggott had organized his life quite perfectly. How could he possibly fail? He had done his work, learned his lessons, and his reward the finest string of classic racehorses in England at his disposal. His new wife would soften the hard, one-dimensional scale of his life, later giving him daughters he would adore. It is true that he had the young man's urge for a son, the mixture of ego and hope which affects those who believe they have something special to offer England. He bet a rival jockey that his first child would be a son. For someone who so regularly kept connections and backers waiting anxiously along the final furlong, Piggott became surprisingly restive when his wife lingered over the birth of the first child. She was two weeks late, which was, to be fair, as tardy as any late run he ever made on the back of Petite Etoile.

At Chester the father-to-be rode one of his more reckless races in the Grosvenor Stakes. He got in a mêlée involving Doug Smith, Harry Carr, and Scobie Breasley, and all four jockeys were shown the film of the race. Piggott watched somewhat sheepishly. He was cautioned by the stewards. Then he went to his hotel and took a call. It was from his wife.

'Lester,' she said, 'it's a girl and we are both doing well.'

Piggott paid up the fiver with a promptness which did not go without comment. The baby was called Maureen. Tracy followed five years later. Maureen, say friends, is most like her father. She is more introverted than her sister, more obsessed with the need to succeed. Experts predict an outstanding career for her in three-day events. She has already received international recognition. Piggott, when he has time, watches her with a rapt, proud, but not uncritical eye. His advice is sparing, and more effective for that. Vincent O'Brien once underlined this point neatly enough when he said, 'Lester Piggott doesn't say much, but when he speaks, you listen.'

Susan Piggott is candid about the fact that the pressure her husband lives under can cause eruptions.

> He shouts sometimes – when we quarrel we raise our voices pretty loud – but he is never surly. The Piggott you see on the box is just an image because he doesn't like the limelight. But he's not made of stone. He is untemperamental and terribly down to earth, really. A lot of myths have gathered around him and somehow they have stuck; like him being so silent because he is deaf, and winning because he can't hear what's going on around him. He is deaf, but it doesn't hinder or help him and I rarely notice it. It is greatly exaggerated. Like the stories that he is mean. With presents he is a perfectly normal husband and father and the girls are terribly fond and proud of him. Mind you, they enjoy the odd time he's been beaten by a woman jockey. Then the horses are part of him and he really has a special insight into them. He actually can communicate with them as if they were humans.

There is a special quality apparent in Susan Piggott when she speaks of her husband. You could talk about pride, respect, admiration for his unique talent but this is not usual among people like the Piggotts, who operate on the basis that actions speak more eloquently than words; in the end you have to say the quality we are looking at is a fierce love. It is the love for a man who is demonstrably strong and capable. For Susan Piggott there has been from the start a need to offer great support and an extraordinary level of understanding. When a family friend like John Morgan laughingly suggests that the slices carved by Lester Piggott at Sunday lunch may be fine if you have to make the weight in the morning, but mere flesh and blood mortals could do with a little more, there is laughter from the Piggotts, not least from the man himself. But Susan Piggott carries deep fears about the physical sacrifices her husband makes. In an unguarded moment she once confessed, 'I heard somewhere that Lester was slowly killing himself with the wasting and it worried me so much, but I insist he goes to regular medicals and the results always say he is very fit.'

In their comfortable modern bungalow outside Newmarket (also called Florizel after their first house) with its spacious garden and swimming-pool, Susan Piggott tries to safeguard the unspoken fears she shares with the wives of all men who do dangerous work. The life-styles may be different, but like the women in miners' and trawlermen's houses she knows that at any time the alarm could be raised. She has nursed Piggott through a score of injuries and one of her worst moments was watching Durtal charging towards the Epsom rails with her husband trailing hopelessly behind. When not devoting her time to him she works with great industry for the Injured Jockeys' Fund.

The first crisis of their married life came in Derby week of 1962. Piggott was banned for six weeks and Staffordshire trainer Bob Ward received a life suspension, which was subsequently lifted. Piggott was adjudged 'not to have tried' on a horse called Ione, an odds-on favourite in a seller at Lincoln. Ward had another runner, Polly Macaw, in the race and – the outcome can easily be guessed – Polly Macaw romped it. It looked terrible. The trainer declared:

I have seen Piggott ride stronger, but he eased up because he saw no point in thrashing a horse which he realized had no chance of beating Polly Macaw. I told Piggott several times that Polly Macaw was the best of the two horses, but he insisted on riding for the owner of Ione, Mr Grainger. I know the race looked bad as things turned out. It's a pity Piggott didn't keep the horse going harder. It was ridiculous for Ione to be odds-on overnight favourite. He had won only once and was proved a short runner.'

Perhaps the fact of lasting significance to emerge from the whole murky affair was that in the early sixties Piggott had become so much more than a champion jockey. He was irresistible to punters. The Ione affair was so startling because it flew in the face of all that Piggott had done before. His problems had come almost exclusively from an overdeveloped urge to win.

He was, the punters believed, one man about whom they could be sure. Put him on some mediocre nag and who knows what unlikely sparks he could kindle by the power of his riding, his relentless search for the right centre of gravity. He might squeeze out a victory otherwise unthinkable. The business at Lincoln arrested his flow of success and raised new questions about him. The force of his racing personality, the swiftly-revived momentum of his career later that year, would repair the damage to his relationship with the public quickly enough. But he was not that easy to live with for the six weeks of idleness.

It was the summer of 1954 all over again, but with the comfort that on this occasion he wasn't being kept off the back of Never Say Die. Willie Snaith took Piggott's Derby ride, Young Lochinvar, but could make no impression on a field led home by the Never Say Die colt, Larkspur. Piggott morosely contemplated a long list of lost winners. But there were some consolations. Unlike 1954, he didn't feel so rootless, so lost. He had the comfort of a wife he could talk to in the confidence that she understood his moods. He was intrigued by his infant daughter. His family gave him a new balance, a new perspective. He also knew that Noel Murless would wait.

Noel Murless had a string of horses which would satisfy the needs of the most demanding rider, at least for the next three or four years. Already Murless had delivered a string of astonishing quality to Piggott: Crepello, Petite Etoile, Carrozza, St Paddy, and Primera.

Of all the horses Piggott has ridden, Primera has a special place. Piggott loved the colt's sharp intelligence and willingness to perform any feat of courage on a racetrack. Primera had much of his glory stolen by that outrageous grandstander, the glamorous Petite Etoile, but his work in 1959 could hardly have been more spectacular. He won he Ebor and the Prince of Wales Stakes and came within a length of carrying the Arc de Triomphe. 'Primera always knew when I was around,' said Piggott. 'Horses get that way when you spend so much time with them. But Primera was something special – a character who seemed to give me his own sort of welcome. The great thing about him was that he always tried his heart out.'

No one has known more intensely than Piggott the exhilaration and then the sudden, stomach-pounding blows of the game. Throughout his career the two sensations seem to have been in fierce juxtaposition.

1961 serves as a perfect example. In the spring he felt sure he was heading for another Derby win. It would be his fifth Derby win – at twenty-five. The potential achievement stretched the imagination. The vehicle would be Pinturischio. He had done no better than fourth in the Two Thousand Guineas, but Murless and Piggott concluded that the colt had exciting ground for improvement. Piggott still vividly recalls the anger he felt when he walked into Pinturischio's box one spring morning, some weeks before the Derby. The colt was shattered. He had been doped. 'It was reported that the dopers got in through a hole in the stable roof,' Piggott said. 'It was done much more simply than that. People who dope horses should be shot. Travelling at speed on a horse which has been doped is very dangerous. If a jockey was killed the dopers should be tried for manslaughter.' When the facts had been established it was as though Warren Place had come under artillery fire. Murless was white-faced, speechless with disgust. A trainer knows the natural hazards of bringing on a classic colt. Murless had nursed Crepello to two classic wins in the knowledge that he was walking along a precipice. Every plan, every aspiration for Crepello could have been dashed by one false stride – but that was the game, the glory and the pain of it. This crime was something else.

But racing is like life. It puts men down when they think they have the world at their feet and then, when they are down, it lifts them up, magically. It happened for Murless and Piggott at Doncaster in September, on a good, important day – the day of the St Leger. It was their chance to redeem a blank season in the classics, but the outlook was not that good. Their hopes surrounded the colt Aurelius, son of the Queen's stallion, Aureole. In the spring Aurelius had been utterly upstaged by the proud Pinturischio; although he had benefitted from the vacuum left by the stricken star, he was still quite a way from stardom when the St Leger came.

Aurelius had a chance, of course. A hungry Piggott was up, and this alone kept the odds down. Aurelius was a respectable 9–2. Piggott had been drawing the money of the small doubtful punter and the housewife who, despite the lean year, still saw him as something of a cross between Gary Cooper and Frank Sinatra. The French colt Dicta Drake was considered favourite at 6–4.

Piggott's luck appeared to change right from the moment the starting gate flew up. Just Great, the second favourite, stood firm; his jockey, Scobie Breasley, appalled, flashed his whip, but Just Great had no taste for the action. The field was a hundred yards clear of the gate when Just Great finally moved forward, tentatively. Breasley, with an expression of comic disgust on his face, trotted round the course. Piggott's second piece of good fortune was that Dicta Drake's jockey Max Garcia was in a somewhat reckless mood. Aurelius's great strength was his stamina, a potent weapon in the 1¾ mile St Leger, and Murless had sent in a pacemaker, Hunter's Song. The pace sizzled. Five furlongs out Hunter's Song yielded to a more serious contender. Garcia, who had expressed contempt for the field, sent Dicta Drake surging for the post. Piggott wanted to believe it but for a few seconds he couldn't quite – Garcia had galloped straight into a trap, a long straight of a trap which gave him plenty of time to curse himself as Piggott inexorably tightened the noose. A furlong and a half out Piggott kicked the plank from beneath Garcia's feet. Piggott, working with his meticulous sense of balance, drove Aurelius into the lead. The locals got excited when their townsman Joe Sime produced Bounteous for a strong late run. But Sime didn't have an elephant gun. It would have taken that to stop Piggott rescuing his season. Aurelius came in by three-quarters of a length.

Susan Piggott once said, 'Lester is astonishingly brave about losing. I don't say he doesn't feel it, but he won't show it any more than he will jump around when he's won.

I do get a bit annoyed when people criticize Lester. I see him as a perfectly ordinary man.'

For an ordinary man it was spectacular stock-taking in September 1961. He had a wife who might have been custom-made. He had a beautiful daughter. It seemed nothing, not even a doping gang, could stop him winning at least one big one.

11 Riding Out Alone

Few words are more poignant than the heartfelt regrets of people who have let something great slip through their fingers. 'I never realized how lucky I was,' they say. 'I took things for granted ... I let it all slide away ... if I only could have my time over again.' It can be the epilogue of a great career, a great marriage, a great life. Because racing is the way it is, which is to say fleeting and avaricious and given to much envy, there were many who waited keenly for this speech in the early summer of 1967. They wanted to hear it on the lips of Lester Piggott.

The majority feeling was that Piggott had finally done that which he had been promising since his days as a curt, impatient and deceptively cherub-faced schoolboy. They said that the boy wonder had raced beyond himself, committed an act which was as arrogant as it was suicidal. How, for heavens sake, could Lester Piggott turn his back on Noel Murless? Biting the hand that feeds you is one thing, but this was dismembering oneself. It was seen as an unlikeable mixture of disloyalty and ingratitude, perhaps the perfect example of a point which had been made for so long, that Lester Piggott's extraordinary level of self-interest would one day undo him. It had done so already, went the argument. Where was the great Piggott without the best trainer in England? He had gone thirty-one races without a win. (Most jockeys would say that going thirty-one races without a win was no reason to seek out a gas oven.)

But for Piggott, certainly, it represented something of a journey into the desert. Where would the classic winners come from? Murless had slammed the door on Warren Place, declaring, 'We have been together for many years and we have had many notable successes. But I have to take this stand. Lester was simply not going to play ducks and drakes with me. I have no regrets at my decision.'

Piggott must have had regrets as he began to work in this harsh new world, alone but for the support of a strong-minded young wife. Never before had a great jockey declared that he could live on his wits; that the force of his own talent and ability to read form and pick up the best mounts was enough to insulate himself against failure. Archer, Donoghue, and Richards had never thought of that, not even at the peak of their careers. Jockeys had gained great celebrity and financial rewards, but they were still physically small men with a feudal habit of touching their caps. Piggott was curling his lip at this. He was saying that he had lifted himself above any master and retainer relationship. Owners and trainers needed him quite as much as he needed them. In racing it was a breath-taking conception. Even Piggott's father, who believed in his son's talent perhaps more than any man alive, advised caution. Years later Keith Piggott confirmed, 'I advised Lester against it. I just didn't see how he could afford to leave Noel Murless and give up all those excellent horses. I said it was rash but I could see on his face that he had made up his mind. Oh, he was determined.'

It appeared that Piggott wanted the freedom to pick from the field, then fall back on Warren Place if his speculations proved unprofitable. It seems probable that this was Piggott's idea of a perfect situation, but he was not allowed to enjoy the possibility for long.

Murless, the gaunt, restrained man whose passions ran deep, snipped the life-line. He lured the leading Australian jockey, George Moore, to Warren Place, and by way of an introductory gift had presented him with the winners of the One Thousand and Two Thousand Guineas and the Derby. It didn't help Piggott's mood that Royal Palace, the outstanding colt of 1967, had not struck him as a particularly good reason to linger at Warren Place the previous autumn. In exchange for the Two Thousand Guineas and the Derby

Piggott might have considered doffing his cap for perhaps another year.

Another Australian, Ron Hutchinson, was setting a brisk early pace in the Jockey's Championship. Was Piggott's empire crumbling? Was the title he had won in 1960, 1965, and 1966 going the same way as the great horses of Warren Place?

The questions and rumours buzzed relentlessly. Racing may be a wonderfully exciting world, filled with characters of extraordinary contrasts, but it is a closed place where jealousies sprout like fungus in a damp room. Robert Sangster, who in the 1970s was to make revolutionary strides in the organization of a bloodstock empire, once made this point vividly:

> Individually, there are so many marvellous people in racing. I find trainers and jockeys the salt of the earth, but I have to admit that the moment someone begins to show real success there is a tendency to put him down, belittle him. One example is when, shortly after we won the Derby with The Minstrel, I overheard a lady, a wife of a Jockey Club Steward, asking her companion in a very loud voice: 'Do you really think this fellow Sangster is good for racing?' Certainly someone like Lester Piggott would get a backlash, a sort of resentment. He is a very strong individual and of course he has had all this fabulous success. So he becomes a target. Knock him and you may disguise a little bit the fact that you haven't been having much success.

Piggott's critics were saying it was over now. And if it wasn't over, at least he wouldn't be lording it quite so much. After the succulent years there would be poorer cuts for the Long Fella. The critics would have done better to consider one important aspect of his style: his mastery of the art of coming from behind.

The reason which finally forced Piggott to risk the cream of Warren Place could hardly have been such a short-term, one-off factor as the superiority of Vincent O'Brien's Valoris to Murless's 1966 Oaks contender Varinia. Although this opinion was put forward by a lot of people it scarcely seems realistic and even at the time Piggott insisted it had no bearing on his decision. He merely said that Valoris was the final nudge along a road he had been travelling for some time.

> I was riding Right Noble for O'Brien in the Derby and I was hopeful of repeating the Epsom Double. I had landed for Murless in 1957. No one outside knew, but there had been a number of crises between us earlier and it was as well the break came when it did. It meant I would not be able to ride many of the best horses, but I was increasingly in demand.

Murless confirmed that there had been growing tension behind the scenes; sometimes Murless's caution had come into conflict with Piggott's more aggressive spirit.

Piggott knew the risks. He also knew how much gold there was waiting for the brave and talented prospector in England, France, Ireland, Germany, Scandanavia, India, Hong Kong, even Australia. Jet travel was pushing back the horizons spectacularly. Racing had grown, and Piggott was growing with it. Over a decade later the American prodigy Steve Cauthen, sitting outside the jockeys' room on a soft summer's evening at Windsor, said:

> We've reached the age of the international jockey, when people don't think anything of flying someone six thousand miles for the big race. I'm thrilled to be involved in this. It appeals to me to race in Germany one day, England the next. It also makes you a far more complete rider. In one summer in England I've learned so much.

The Six Million Dollar Kid was right of course, but he was merely saying things that Piggott had thought ten years earlier. The difference was that Cauthen was toasted for his boldness, Piggott growled at for his arrogance.

Piggott had made a discovery which can elude the most gifted. He had learned how important it was to place a value on your talent. If you did not try to establish that value, he had concluded, others would never do it for you, unless, perhaps, you happened to brush against one of the great philanthropists. In racing, philanthropists do not come in clusters. Above all a practical man, Piggott had explored all the angles, and radiating through his calculations was a central fact: he was the world's best jockey – and by a distance.

O'Brien and his Valoris had, quite simply, come along at the right time. Valoris was a filly of silky good looks and an action which flowed with a beautiful smoothness. Dermot O'Brien, Vincent's brother and assistant, had bought her at Deauville for £11,000. For Charles Clore, it was an acquisition of obvious class. She was a half-sister to the French Derby winner Val de Loir. Valoris had won the Irish Thousand Guineas with a startling ease, accelerating so sharply that the rest of the field might have been going into reverse.

In the Epsom paddock before the Oaks, Valoris was spellbinding. Her coat glowed. The racing correspondent of *The Times*, a paper not given to hurling adjectives, wrote that Valoris was 'exquisite'. Piggott merely guided her around Epsom, comfortable in the knowledge that he held every significant card. Stan Clayton, who was replacing Piggott on Varinia, moved to the front from the start. Piggott settled easily around fourth place and avoided trouble when, at the half-way stage, Shamrock Queen spilled Joe Mercer. Piggott was floating. The others laboured. At Tattenham Corner, Clayton and Varinia were still in front, but the filly was chugging. Two furlongs out, Piggott and Valoris swept to the front. Piggott described the sensation graphically: 'It was like taking a Maserati past a Mini. Valoris was clearly superior, despite running green.' The crowd was scarcely more voluble. This was partly to do with the formal nature of Valoris's victory, partly a reflection of the fierce tide of feelings which had been flowing against the champion. There was a chill in the air when he brought Valoris to the winners' enclosure.

More seriously, there was a heavy attack from Ireland. It carried far more significance than the jeers from the crowd, which spoilt Piggott's day about as much as a parking ticket might the owner of a Rolls Royce. The attack came from Paddy Prendergast, the trainer who brought on two-year-olds with the touch of an artist. Prendergast had come down heavily on the side of his training colleague Murless. He declared, 'I would never engage Lester Piggott again under any terms. Not for the crown jewels of England.' This was a stinging blow, the first note of censure to bring a flicker of concern to Piggott's brow. The timing was surprising. It was less than twelve months after Prendergast had poured praise on Piggott for his handling of Meadow Court in the Irish Derby. Piggott had held off a fierce challenge from his friend Jimmy Lindley, who had drawn unexpected strength from the English colt Convamore. Two furlongs out Convamore, a 20–1 shot, was into a dangerously smooth rhythm. But the threat dissolved when Piggott applied power. The effect was devastating. Prendergast then said, 'All you can say is that it was another beautiful ride by L. Piggott.'

Piggott could scarcely afford to lose the patronage of a trainer as important as Prendergast. Piggott was filled with respect for O'Brien, but he did not want this respect to spill over into dependence. He didn't want too many public rejections from men of Prendergast's calibre. It would be bad for business.

In July 1967 there were rumours of a reconciliation between Murless and Piggott, the implication being that the latter was suffering from withdrawal symptoms, and did, after all, need the security of a big stable. Piggott denied that there was any question of a new contract, saying brusquely, 'I'm still a freelance.' Murless added, 'Although I'm very fond of Lester, this is out of my hands. It's up to my owners and some are not at all keen after the way he had behaved in leaving.' The partnership would come to life from time to time but never again would there be a joint statement of their genius in an English classic. Murless would have much success with jockeys like Moore, before he was hounded back to Australia by attention from large men with stern faces who showed more than a passing interest in acquiring gambling information; the young Scot, Sandy Barclay; and Geoff Lewis. Indeed, Murless smashed the prize record with more than £200,000 of winnings in the first year of Piggott's absence. But it was true that Murless had reached a level of achievement that was perhaps impossible to maintain against increasing competition; gradually his star would wane as that of Vincent O'Brien would rise.

It is ironic now to think that Piggott was considered the vulnerable one, the partner who would fight impossible odds to maintain his status. Ten years later Murless retired, the old grace clouded somewhat by depression at escalating costs, while Piggott still had some of his greatest triumphs before him. It was no more than he had concluded, unsentimentally, so many years before.

Even though a strained parting was inevitable, Piggott felt obliged to pay his respects, register his gratitude.

Warren Place was run with military precision and Noel knew the potential of every horse in the yard. Of course he was a master trainer. Lots of trainers have had big strings of horses, but they couldn't get them to win. Noel had a marvellous touch. Bringing Crepello through was a magnificent achievement. The colt was only just sound. You could not leave a man like that lightly.

He could scarcely have left Warren Place without making such a tribute, nor without a twinge for all those moments of extraordinary triumph. There were the seven classic wins: Crepello of the flawed magnificence, who might have been the first colt since Bahram to land the triple crown; Carrozza with her gameness in the last furlong of the Oaks; Petite Etoile, the electric lady; poor old St Paddy who ploughed on to win the Derby and St Leger; and Aurelius, who brought the first smiles to Warren Place after the Pinturischio doping. Those were supreme examples of the Murless touch, a touch so smooth, so adept. But there was so much else besides. Twilight Alley was perhaps the most spectacular example of superiority; Piggott had flaunted the great edge he took into the 1963 Ascot Gold Cup. He took it up from the start and the entire field might have been so many puppets, all of whose strings were in his grasp. In his last Royal Ascot with Murless Piggott had nine winners. Each of his eleven years at Warren Place had been starred with major victories.

There were some less uplifting moments, of course. He made regular visits to Magistrates' Courts to defend himself against speeding charges. He was once banned for six months. He drove rather as he rode: if there was daylight he tended to go. He was fined £25 for driving along Hendon Way at 64 mph. He shrugged; he was a busy man. Graham Hill observed Piggott's driving technique one afternoon at the Lotus test track in Norfolk. Hill was deeply impressed by the smooth control and the fast line of Piggott's performance. Less impressed was John Morgan, former *Daily Express* sports editor, who accompanied Piggott on a drive during a rare golfing holiday in the Bahamas. Piggott spotted a short cut which involved crossing several houses'-front lawns and dismantling one clothes line. Of course he took it. The same friend was alarmed when Piggott took him the wrong way down a one-way street in Newmarket. There was much horn-blowing from one motorist. 'What's the problem?' asked Piggott. 'hasn't he got enough room?'

There were also alarms on the course. In 1963 there had been the Casabianca Affair. When Piggott brought home Casabianca at Newbury a spectator claimed that he had badly abused the horse, that he had crossed the line between reminding and inflicting real cruelty. The RSPCA, the great guardian of moral outrage, were drawn into the matter. The allegation was that Piggott had 'soundly thrashed' Casabianca. He denied it of course, repeated his position that he was the best judge of what reserves a horse had left and that it was his professional duty to bring out that which was there. The charge, sniffed Piggott, was 'ridiculous'. Murless agreed:

I don't accept the criticisms. Casabianca is a lazy type of horse. When it gets to the front of the field it thinks the race is over and won and there is nothing left to do. Piggott gave it a smack on the hindquarters, where it doesn't hurt and the horse started forward more in surprise than anything else. That was all. There are jockeys who know how to hurt a horse – under the girth, across the belly – and will do so. But not Piggott. He may wave the whip a lot and certainly he is a determined rider. But cruel – never.

The debate raged for weeks and it would be idle to suggest that this was an isolated incident. Some people are convinced that Piggott is so profoundly ruthless that random cruelty is an inevitable by-product. It is an argument that tends to be advanced by the sentimental, those who idealize the relationship between man and animal. There is no verdict to an argument as emotionally charged as this, but it is perhaps worth noting that two years after the Newbury incident Piggott rode a hard finish on Casabianca to win the Royal Hunt Cup. Again he pushed Casabianca to the limits. It is reasonable to presume that had Piggott inflicted real cruelty on the horse at Newbury the likelihood of reproducing a finish of that quality would have been remote. In the Royal Hunt Cup man and horse seemed to merge into one surging force.

There were some bumps too, in the Murless years. In 1964 he was taken from Longchamp by ambulance. He spent the night in an expensive clinic, bruised and sour after falling along with two riders in the Prix Henri Delamarre. Piggott wore the aggrieved expression of the downtrodden innocent. The culprit was his much-respected international rival, Yves St Martin. He was banned for a month.

It could be said that Piggott had seen it all and knew it all when he left Murless. He knew the pinnacles of racing achievement and he knew the bad times, too. He knew the pain of rejection and, privately, he would claim a certain persecution by the authorities. He knew broken bones, the pain of wasting, and the endless cycle which came with winning domestic championships and competing in the front rank in Ireland and France.

Another point obscured by the controversy of his break with Murless was the benefit he was spreading among his brother jockeys. Piggott's successor at Warren Place, Moore, was reputed to have received a retainer of £20,000 plus. It was an unprecedented price to pay for the service of a stable jockey and inevitably the good men operating on the level immediately below Piggott felt the warm glow. Experienced jockeys like Ron Hutchinson and Joe Mercer, coming boys like Pat Eddery and Willie Carson, would all be offered better terms by trainers suddenly alert to the dangers of defection.

For Piggott, though, there was the more pressing

personal question of how much he would benefit from the break. It would take more than one Oaks victory to answer. What price would he pay for the ride on Valoris? 1967 started brightly enough. Piggott won some big races in Australia and returned to Newmarket with a good tan and considerable confidence. But it was not shared by one of his great admirers, the Midlands bookie Fred Binns, who lengthened the odds on Piggott retaining the jockeys' title. 'I'm not sure that Lester's new arrangement can make him champion again,' he said. 'He's a great jockey, of course, but he's taken on the whole racing world. He's given himself a hell of a job.'

Piggott had a sprinkling of winners in the first week of the new season, but soon enough the misgivings of Fred Binns seemed to have been built on solid foundations. Piggott entered his losing run of thirty-one and the racing world shook its head. Piggott simply rode on, his self-confidence ungrazed.

Other people were much more aware of the failures than I was. In the first few days I rode four winners. But horses can be baffling creatures and a number of well-fancied ones ran badly. Racing is the way it is, and most people who bet heavily finish up the way they do because horses, like humans, have their off days. I have been told by trainers hundreds of times that mounts for which they have booked me were bound to win but I've known within seconds of mounting that they had no chance. Others give you the feeling that they are feeling good. There is no explanation why the form of many of them is so unpredictable. I have won races on horses which looked like donkeys. Generally a horse that is well has a bloom in the coat and is not fat. There are moderate animals who invariably run up to form. Then there are the good but flashy ones who leave the owner and trainer puzzled, the jockey stranded and the bookmakers happy.

There was a strange twist to the ending of Piggott's lean run. It came on the back of Royal Saint, Piggott fighting off a strong late challenge from a horse called Whirled. The race was at Newbury, the home course of his youth. The trainer was Noel Murless! Royal Saint's owner, Mrs Vera Hue-Williams, had dug in her heels on the matter of who should ride her horse. Her attitude was positive, practical, and no doubt a little selfish. She wanted the best for her horse's chances of winning. She didn't want the nicest jockey, the one with the best developed sense of personal loyalty. She wanted the man best qualified to get her in the winners' enclosure. This meant that she wanted Lester Piggott.

So, of much more lasting significance, did the 27-year-old trainer Fulke Johnson Houghton. He had a colt called Ribocco. It would be on Ribocco that Piggott would prove beyond doubt that he could survive without Noel Murless, though not without suffering. Even Piggott must have winced at the splendour of Murless's assault on the 1967 classics. Like a conveniently-placed row of skittles, the first classics tumbled to Murless and Moore. The Australian jockey had quickly proved that he could translate his eminence down under into English success, and his performance in the Two Thousand Guineas alerted the sceptical to an impressive temperament. The French colt Taj Dewan applied blistering pressure along the last two hundred yards. It was an early, biting test of Moore's mettle, and he simply sailed through the examination. Royal Palace had looked something less than invincible in the paddock, sweating badly and giving the general impression that Newmarket on Two Thousand Guineas day was some way from being his favourite bag of oats. Moore settled the colt down well and when Taj Dewan came with his late burst there was not a hint of concern. Moore eased Royal Palace home by inches. In the One Thousand Guineas Moore had a more comfortable time, winning on Fleet.

Moore therefore came to Epsom the conqueror. Royal Palace was the firmest of the favourites, at 7–4. Ribocco was 22–1. He had been an impressive two-year-old, a viable Derby prospect, but his approach to Epsom had been less than inspiring. There had been a string of morale-sapping defeats at Newmarket, Chester and Lingfield. Even so, there was a willingness to dismiss this depressing evidence as the field swung round Tattenham Corner into the straight. It was clear that Piggott was riding another beautiful Derby.

He had taken Ribocco wide of trouble at the corner and had placed him perfectly for a run along the centre of the course. A furlong out he was alongside Royal Palace. Piggott was doing for Ribocco all that he had done for Never Say Die, Carrozza, Petite Etoile, Crepello and St Paddy along this same stretch of turf.

By then Moore had learned self-possession. He had not come to England a novice; he had won a few things, and that day there was no question about the most crucial factor of all: Royal Palace was faster than Ribocco and was finishing more powerfully. Moore kept Royal Palace's rhythm, applied a gentle 'reminder' and, despite the explosions of sound from the grandstand, it was a defeat for Warren Place. Royal Palace came in by two and a half lengths. But Piggott's attack had not been halted, merely delayed. He pressed forward again, brilliantly, in the Irish Derby.

Once again it was Piggott versus Moore along the final furlong, but this time Piggott had the means to assert his genius. Moore was cool and professional but all those on the great moor of The Curragh knew that against him was a man exploring the utmost limits of a remarkable talent. It was a dramatic race, grimly so for the Irish contender Royal Sword. Seven furlongs from home Royal Sword snapped a foreleg and spread-eagled. He was put down immediately. Scobie Breasley on Dart Board narrowly averted disaster, righting the colt after a glancing collision with the stricken Royal Sword. Breasley claimed that had it not been for that incident he would have been up with Piggott at the finish, but the racing commentary then and throughout the summer of 1967 revolved almost exclusively around Moore and Piggott. They were fighting a duel that hinged on Piggott's ability to prove himself under the fiercest pressure he ever suffered. Two furlongs out Moore, aboard Sucaryl, went into the lead. Piggott still had much to do, ground to find, gaps to pass through, but he could sense that Ribocco was ready to atone for his failure of pace along the last yards of the Epsom Derby. Ribocco responded beautifully to every subtle shift of Piggott's weight. A furlong out Ribocco was at Sucaryl's heels and for a time that seemed interminable to Fulke Johnson Houghton Piggott kept him there. It was as though Piggott was taunting Moore, punishing him for the impertinence of assuming his crown.

Piggott allowed Moore to suffer a while. The Australian's whip flashed but it was the gesture of a desperate man. At the last possible minute Piggott opened the throttle. Ribocco won with a length to spare.

After the race Piggott said, 'I couldn't get to the outside like at Epsom. But I didn't have to sit still on him either. He was sneaking through openings you wouldn't think a mouse could take.'

Moore, drained by the tension of the finish, asked Piggott: 'Did you always look like getting me?'

'Sure,' said Piggott. 'I knew we had it a long way out.'

The 1967 Irish Derby merged into the stream of Piggott successes long ago, but he will never forget that day on The Curragh, the roar of the Irish throng sounding in his ears. The outcome of the race clearly told him something he had always believed: there was no way Lester Piggott could be kept away from the great prizes.

His supporters could draw a similar degree of pleasure from a far less spectacular occasion, a night meeting at Leicester a few weeks after the Irish Derby. Piggott brought in the modest Moonbeam, his 2,000th winner. Only seven others had attained the mark – Fred Archer, Scobie Breasley, George Fordham, Billy Nevett, Gordon Richards, Doug and Eph Smith. Piggott was pushing relentlessly to the front of racing history, and would keep his title for another five years, after which he was able to feel he had made his point. With the title threat under control, if not removed, he could address himself to the last big challenge of 1967. He could perhaps win an English classic, a prospect which had seemed remote in the spring. He could win the St Leger, for the third time, again putting George Moore to the test. There was nothing personal between them; Piggott claimed that he found the Australian likeable and professional. Moore was simply in the way.

With two hundred yards to go in the 1967 St Leger Moore, on the royal horse Hopeful Venture, was duelling with the

Italian hope, Ruysdael II, when Piggott came cruising past to finish by one and a half lengths. For Ribocco's American owner, Charles Englehard, it meant the prize-winning record for an English-trained colt. The previous record-holder was the 1966 Derby winner Charlottown, who brought in £101,209. Ribocco beat that record by £20,000. Engelhard, a member of the New York Jockey Club with world-wide bloodstock interests, was suitably grateful. He gave Piggott generous gifts and later showed his gratitude in other ways. Soon, for instance, he was to own a yearling called Nijinsky....

There would be no heartfelt regrets by Piggott at the end of 1967, no adjusting the sails for the safe harbour of a big stable. He remained champion jockey of England. He had become a man able to look down from a high vantage point and pick classic winners out of the pack. His mood that autumn was understandably good and for once he made little attempt to conceal the fact. He said of his fifth title:

It means nothing to me in terms of money but, in terms of satisfaction, being champion in 1967 is worth a great deal more to me than usual. It's an answer to everyone who said at the start of the year that I was finished. It's a very fickle game, racing. If you don't win all the time they are quick to say you are on the way out. It's the same to some extent in other sports but in racing there is so much money – and this makes it worse.

There was a touch of bitterness in Piggott's words. He had learned the hard lesson of all champions, that there are two kinds of friends – those who are knocking on the door of the dressing-room the night you have lost the title, and the others, more numerous, who are at that moment already pouring champagne in the noisy room just down the corridor.

His good luck was that he was only thirty-two. In the future there would be more titles than friends.

12 The Irish Connection

Some partnerships do not spring up by chance, accidents of time and circumstances. They are a blending of known strengths by men who demand excellence in themselves and seek it out in others. That has always been the basis of Piggott–O'Brien Ltd. They saw in each other an impatience with anything less than perfection. Vincent O'Brien could never have lured Lester Piggott away from Noel Murless merely with the bait of one filly, even one as pretty and as fast as Valoris. There had to be back-up. There had to be a feeling in Piggott that O'Brien could build on past achievements, maintain a momentum which would lead him to a domination of European training as profound as Piggott's own mastery of European riding. Piggott had to be sure of his supply lines. He was playing poker with his career and he needed good cards. He weighed O'Brien's situation carefully, and concluded that O'Brien was about to take off into a new level of flight.

Already, O'Brien had opened and closed one brilliant career. His hold over National Hunt racing had become almost complete by the mid fifties. The short, always immaculately-dressed Irishman, who might have been taken for an upper-echelon business executive on his many trips to the rich breeding country of Kentucky, had one day reviewed his days among the hurdlers and the steeplechasers. It was an exercise scarcely designed to undermine his self-confidence. Inevitably, he found himself asking the questions that sooner or later present themselves to every successful man: What more can I do? What is there left? How can I keep my edge?

One has only to skim O'Brien's National Hunt record to grasp the scale of his problem – and understand his need for a break, a new dimension. He had raided Cheltenham as rapaciously as any Viking taking an English pleasure cruise. He had won four Cheltenham Gold Cups, three Champion Hurdles. To the Irish throng who came to the Cotswolds with wads of banknotes he was a wizard. Magically, his horses always came to the great festival glossy and filled with power. On one occasion an amiable Irish monsignor said 'Bless you, my son, and bless your horses.' An Englishman hearing this groaned, 'Good God, he scarcely needs the Holy Spirit.'

In the years 1953–5 O'Brien annexed Aintree, winning the Grand National with Early Mist, Royal Tan and Quare Times. He was described as 'a perfectionist and a worrier, grey before he was forty'. He had shown the value he put on good horsemanship, removing his brother Phonsie, a brave though somewhat reckless rider, from his National candidates, and installing Bryan Marshall and Pat Taafe, two of the greatest jump jockeys who ever lived.

It was clear to O'Brien in the late fifties that there was nothing left to win in National Hunt racing. He had to move on. He would have a go at the flat. Almost immediately, he produced Ballymoss. As an opening statement it was like coming in from the street, landing a world title fight, and delivering a knock-out blow in the first round. Ballymoss had just one misfortune in an astonishing career: he encountered Lester Piggott and Crepello on English Derby Day. Ballymoss, largely responsible for anouncing the quality of a Vincent O'Brien just emerging from Grand National glory, won the Irish Derby, the St Leger, the Eclipse Stakes, the Coronation Cup, the King George VI and Queen Elizabeth Stakes, and the Prix de l'Arc de Triomphe. Classic victories began to fall around O'Brien's feet as thickly as grouse on the Glorious Twelfth. There was Larkspur (1962 Derby), Long Look (1965 Oaks), Valoris and Glad Rags (1966 Thousand Guineas). O'Brien could have retired in 1967 safe in the knowledge that few trainers would ever have the audacity to dream of matching his achievements.

Retirement was the last thought in his head when he patrolled the Tipperary gallops early in 1968. He was just fifty. When his eyes swept the gallops they saw a fine long string of beautifully bred animals. He had rich patrons on either side of the Atlantic, and as this new year unfolded his gaze centred on a superb bay colt. The colt thrilled him more than any animal he had known since his days as an amateur rider in the early 1940s. The colt had power and wonderfully sleek lines and when he moved into top gear, well, it was quite extraordinary. The sight of this colt flying across the turf deeply moved O'Brien, a man who had turned the training of racehorses into an exact science. The colt was Sir Ivor. He was Lester Piggott's most spectacular prize on the flight from Warren Place. But he was no easy prize. He was a gem which had to be worked with some difficulty, and along the way there had to be much thought and some delicate decisions.

Even the initial decision to select him as the classic ride was unusually complicated. Piggott's father-in-law Sam Armstrong was rapturous about the classic potential of his two-year-old Petingo. Naturally enough, he wanted his son-in-law up. There was no horse so good that it would not benefit from the handling of the best available jockey. Piggott went to Armstrong's St Gatien stables, just down the road from his home in Newmarket, and rode Petingo at work. He liked the colt. It had a good smooth action and genuine pace. In other years he would have gladly snapped up Sam Armstrong's offer, but 1968 was no ordinary year.

From the moment Piggott first mounted Sir Ivor he sensed that this might be a year to contrast with all the others.

> The first time I got on Sir Ivor I realized it was a superb horse. The feeling I got was similar to the one I got when I first rode Crepello. It's a lovely feeling. It's the knowledge that you've got real power at your disposal. It gives you freedom of action, a lot of options if things get difficult.

Sir Ivor, by Gaylor, out of Attica, was bred in Kentucky and cost Raymond Guest, who was then American Ambassador in Dublin, $43,000. He was bought for Guest by Bull Hancock, an important name in the US bloodstock market. Hancock ran the famous Claiborne Stud Farm. He bought Sir Ivor at the Keeneland Bloodstock Sales. He knew the genius of the breeder, Hal Price Headley. Headley had turned a $500 start into a $5 million empire before his death. He had a touch, and Hancock believed he saw it clearly in this colt, Sir Ivor. The colt was sent immediately to O'Brien and Guest drove down to Cashel from Dublin. There was the soft, green countryside and at the end of the journey there was a sight to lift the spirit of any man, the beautiful colt who looked poised to beat the world. Sir Ivor started modestly at The Curragh, finishing sixth in the Tyros Stakes. His reputation had spread through Ireland and he had started the race a joint 3–1 favourite. But O'Brien was not dismayed. Sir Ivor would come on in the season. The talent was very close to the surface. There would be a little mining, a little patience, and then the diamonds would come spilling out into the sunshine. O'Brien was sure of this – and so was Piggott. Four weeks later Sir Ivor won the Probationers' Stakes at The Curragh, holding off Mistigo, winner of the Tyros Stakes, by a neck.

By mid September Sir Ivor was beginning to flow. There would be doubts about his stamina right up to the English Derby – and even after that they would linger, at least in Lester Piggott's mind – but the class and the speed were evident enough in the seven-furlong National Stakes, also at The Curragh. Over the last furlong he was dramatic, irresistible. The favourite, Candy Cane, floundered three lengths behind. Society, in third place, was another four lengths away. It was the first irrefutable public evidence of lacerating speed. O'Brien's vision of Sir Ivor had suddenly come into focus for the rest of the racing world.

The colt would go to Longchamp and the one-mile Grand Criterium. There was £30,000 of prize money at stake but, more important on a day when a strong wind tossed the chestnut trees of the Champs Elysées and driving rain left the great course heavy, was the opportunity to examine thoroughly Sir Ivor's ability to stay. Piggott was at his most thoughtful with so much at stake. He kept Sir Ivor covered right into the last furlong, and then released him. He might have been releasing a bow-string. Sir Ivor was a star. He flew beyond Pola Bella and Timmy My Boy. The French gasped.

Sir Ivor wintered in Italy, almost in the shadow of the leaning tower of Pisa. He was clearly worth cossetting. The smooth surface of Sir Ivor glowed and rippled in the pale winter sunshine. He returned to Ireland looking every inch a champion and the first gallops in Tipperary convinced O'Brien that the sojourn in Italy had been a shrewd investment. There seemed just the one threat to his chances in the Two Thousand Guineas. It was Petingo, the colt Piggott's father-in-law still believed would dominate the summer. Sir Ivor carried Ascot's Guineas trial, but Petingo fired a riposte in the Craven Stakes at Newmarket. The balance was nicely reflected by the odds on the morning of the Guineas: Sir Ivor was 11–8, Petingo 9–4.

The coolness of Piggott, his refusal to depart from his precise conception of the needs of a horse in any particular race, had long become commonplace in racing. What Piggott achieved in the 1968 Guineas was a striking example of this quality. A lesser man might have been panicked, or at least made uncertain, by So Blessed's scorching exit from the stalls. For three furlongs Piggott idled towards the rear. Of course he had done his laborious homework, measuring precisely calculating time and distance, and feeding into the figures and his hunches the decisive factor of Sir Ivor's capacity to produce a sudden, space-consuming turn of speed. A furlong out Sam Armstrong's winter-long hope flickered into life, but it was rapidly quenched as Sir Ivor came hurtling out of the pack. Petingo was utterly stretched, whereas there might have been a cushion of air beneath Sir Ivor's hooves. He was completely effortless in the quickening of his stride.

In terms of physical distance Sir Ivor had won by a length and a half. Morally, he had won by the width of Newmarket Heath. He would take to Epsom a legion of supporters, many of whom were moved not so much by the acceptable prospect of financial gain but the emotional kick of attaching their hopes to a colt whose speed and grace touched deeper responses. Inevitably, the doubts about stamina persisted. There was, after all, more speed than stamina in his blood. But the speed of his finish surely reflected too much power to be dissolved by the extra distance. The finish was a rapier thrust, but also a sign of inherent power.

Raymond Guest was appalled by the collision of dates which meant that he would not be able to see his colt carry his reputation to Epsom. He had an important public duty as US Ambassador attending the opening of a John F. Kennedy Memorial in Wexford. There was one powerful comfort, though; the previous summer Guest had made a good bet with William Hill. He had £500 or Sir Ivor to win. At 100–1. Bookmakers had looked drawn at Newmarket after the Guineas, and they had good reason.

For years the appeal of Piggott had been slashing into profit margins and, in some cases, turning black ink into red so dramatically that there were scores of bookmakers who could say that they had been ruined by Lester Piggott. It was little consolation that he worked his relentless destruction without discrimination down the years. Piggott had reduced the variables of gambling drastically. In 1968 he was on a flier for the Derby. Derby Day was not something the bookmakers really wanted to think about, nor was there any relief for them when the day arrived. They looked at Sir Ivor in the paddock and groaned. He looked stronger than ever before. There was not a hint of lather. His coat glowed. O'Brien saw three possible problems. The first two, Remand, ridden by Joe Mercer, and Connaught, a son of St Paddy and the mount of Noel Murless's new stable jockey, Sandy Barclay, could surely be handled by Piggott. The other fear was that Sir Ivor might get too excited by the lengthy pre-race rituals. O'Brien could do something about this. He posted his head lad, Maurice O'Callaghan, at the paddock and gave firm instructions that after the post-parade canter Sir Ivor must be led gently to the start. 'I did fear that Sir Ivor might get a bit stirred up during the parade,' said

O'Brien, 'but the sight of Maurice and the sound of his voice would help to reassure him and calm his excitability.'

It was a small detail but it was on such details that O'Brien had built his empire. Many fine colts had dissolved before the great heaving crowds of Epsom. It is bad enough to fail in a race round which your year has revolved, but how much worse if that failure could be traced to a small oversight. So Sir Ivor went to the post in beautiful shape – in sharp contrast to the second favourite, Remand. Joe Mercer was filled with anxiety. In his championship year of 1979 he told me that that day at Epsom still nagged him. He felt it was his great chance of landing the Derby, but going down to the start he realized that something was wrong. In fact a virus was taking hold of the colt, and he didn't run again that summer.

Noel Murless shared the doubts about Sir Ivor's ability to cover one and a half miles and his instructions to young Barclay were more emphatic than they had ever been to Lester Piggott. Barclay was told to make his move early, drive hard for the finish and examine more seriously than ever before the range of O'Brien's star.

Epsom was stunned when Barclay took it up on the descent to Tattenham Corner. Barclay had slipped the field! Coming into the straight Connaught had a five-length lead. Jimmy Lindley, on Atopolis, was prominent at the Corner. Remand was between him and Connaught. Where was Piggott? Lindley wondered, and of course the answer was instantly supplied. Later he recalled, 'He went past me like a flying-machine. He went up to Remand, could have passed him, but to my astonishment Lester took a pull even though Connaught appeared to be uncatchable.'

O'Brien, at the finish, ducked under the rail to get a better view, his binoculars resting on the haunch of a police horse. Remand fell away, but though Sir Ivor's rhythm was perfect it seemed that the great prize had slipped away. Barclay still had it into the last furlong. Piggott guided Sir Ivor to the outside, and then asked Sir Ivor for the finish. For a second there was no response. O'Brien grimaced, but before the expression was formed it was gone; Piggott had conjured it once more. The speed he coaxed from Sir Ivor defied the imagination. The reaction of the crowd was thunderous but delayed.

'Lester has never won a greater or better judged race,' said Jimmy Lindley. 'That was a miracle performance.' The margin was a length and a half.

Sandy Barclay said he believed that there had been no danger a hundred yards from the finish. 'I thought Lester and Sir Ivor must have jumped in the race.'

'He didn't fly immediately,' Piggott commented. 'I pulled him out, but when he went, he went.'

Raymond Guest flew into London that evening. He had with him members of the Kennedy clan, Mrs Teddy Kennedy and Eunice Shriver, and there was the Irish President Eammon de Valera. The great room in the Savoy Hotel was filled with music and laughter. Lester Piggott smoked a huge cigar and smiled. He had done some extraordinary things in his career. But there had been nothing quite like this. He and Sir Ivor were out on their own.

13 A Perfect Year

Going back down the years to 1968, freezing all the moments of triumph at Epsom and Ascot, York and Goodwood, Longchamp and Washington it is bizarre to encounter the fact that it was one of racing's youngest trainers, Fulke Johnson Houghton, who had stood between Lester Piggott and a kind of oblivion. In 1967 Johnson Houghton had, according to majority opinion in racing, given Piggott a lifeline with the Ribocco rides at The Curragh and Doncaster. In 1968 even Piggott's fiercest critics had to accept that Johnson Houghton did not come merely to rescue Piggott; he came to present him with his chance to turn an already glorious season into one as round and as perfect as any sportsman had known since the days of ancient Greece. However, in the summer of 1968 Johnson Houghton's offering did not seem that spectacular. He appeared to be offering little more than a consolation prize. As consolation prizes go, sons of the great Ribot come highly, but Ribero – Johnson Houghton's hope for the Irish Derby – was a poor substitute for Sir Ivor. Vincent O'Brien's policy of granting leading Irish jockey Liam Ward 'home rights' on his best horses meant that Piggott had to look elsewhere for glory in the great race of The Curragh.

No one knew more keenly than Piggott that it was a forlorn search. No one knew so intimately the power of Sir Ivor, that glorious, scarcely perceptible gear-change which left fine rivals far behind. The smiles and the glitter of the big room in the Savoy was a memory now. All eyes fastened on Sir Ivor and Liam Ward. Piggott's instinct would be to dispute the O'Brien rule. Ward was a good jockey, a favourite of The Curragh crowd, but was it not true that Piggott had ridden Sir Ivor quite perfectly? Had it not been a masterpiece of judgement, of sublime timing?

Fulke Johnson Houghton had been a good ally in that critical phase of 1967; Ribocco had given Piggott one of the most vital leg-ups of his life. The fact Ribocco's brother was in a different league was unfortunate, of course. But Piggott had a job to do. He had to take Ribero round The Curragh in good, professional fashion, get him into position – and then? Grit his teeth and wait for Sir Ivor and Liam Ward.

On the form book Ribero's challenge seemed utterly unrealistic. At Ascot he had trundled in twelve lengths behind Connaught and the world knew what had happened to Connaught when Sir Ivor had made the big move at Epsom. Sir Ivor looked as good as ever in the paddock. The Curragh hummed with expectation. All day the road from Dublin had been in that special chaos which with the prospect of a great horse and a great performance. It wasn't just the sporting types of Dublin, of course; they came from all over Europe and North America to see the wonder colt. And from every corner of Ireland. The men of Tipperary brought a special proprietorial pride. The lilting, urgent chatter grew in strength as the field cantered to the start. It took some time to get them started. The tic-tac men flew at their work, flashing the story of the latest betting, and none of their messages interfered with the notion that the work of Ward would be perfunctory.

Piggott had no fears about his ride. Ribero was a tough, undramatic sort and he would give no trouble, show no meanness or agitation. His problem was one shared by all of Sir Ivor's rivals, including the good French colt Val d'Aoste. Ribero simply wasn't quick enough and, ultimately, there was nothing even Lester Piggott could do about that. He could conjure a result, 'nick it' if there was an even spread of talent through the field. But this race had too great a talent in Sir Ivor to be 'nicked'. Piggott would do what he could; what he had done thousands of times before. He would take a horse to the limits of its ability, and shrug his shoulders when it proved insufficient. 'You can only do the best you can; there's no point in trying to find something which isn't there,' he has often said.

Piggott tracked the leaders. He was pleased with the brisk pace. There were doubts about Sir Ivor's stamina. There always would be, he would later claim under fierce criticism. Coming into the straight Giolla Mear and Stitch led with Ribero at their heels. The vast happy crowd saw no reason for concern. Sir Ivor was last but cruising. Ward could scarcely have been more confident. He could work a gear stick as well as Lester Piggott. But, two furlongs out, the race changed – utterly. The crowd was breathless; there was a dramatic change in the demeanour of Liam Ward. He no longer sat still. His arms flailed. His urging seemed desperate – yet Sir Ivor made no move. Ward was not Piggott, but he was a fine, persuasive jockey with a firm, professional touch. Still, there was no surge from Sir Ivor. Piggott recalled his own amazement, and Ward's dawning horror:

'I looked over my shoulder and Sir Ivor was cantering over me. I said to myself, that's it, but all of a sudden Sir Ivor was going back ... what was wrong with him? Who would know?' At Epsom it had been a puff of blue smoke and a sudden flash. Here at The Curragh it was a fizzle.

'He went to pieces on me a furlong out,' Ward said grimly. 'I was glad to see Ribero leading me into the straight, but things certainly didn't work out from there.' Piggott has sensed Sir Ivor's impotence so quickly. His reaction had been the instinctive one of a champion runner who feels the strength leaving his opponent, and who knows that it is time to move, time to turn the screw to his advantage. Piggott drove Ribero beyond Stitch and Giolla Mear and, though Sir Ivor followed, Ward's desperation seemed to radiate out through the crowd. Sir Ivor, 3–1 on, could not win now. Piggott had it. By two lengths.

Ribero's owner, Charles Engelhard, was fishing the Cascapedia River in Canada at the time. He had been doing the same thing the previous year when Piggott brought in Ribocco. Engelhard's racing manager, David McCall, looked like a man who might have some explaining to do. 'He will be bewildered,' said McCall. 'I told him that we would gladly settle for third place.' A result like that was beyond even the terms of Lester Piggott's talent. At first there was a feeling that Sir Ivor had fallen victim to a bug which had been moving briskly about the Cashel stables for the previous ten days. O'Brien and Ward were both dumbfounded. O'Brien eventually said:

It could be the bug, though certainly he showed no signs before the race. We won't know until we get home. If he has not got the bug, maybe he just failed to stay at the pace the race was run. It is a stiff mile and a half and he certainly didn't see it out today. This is the other side of the picture – the defeat that is always waiting for you in racing.

Owner Raymond Guest had learned the ways of a diplomat. He smiled gamely and asked: 'Where is the bar?' One day he would see Sir Ivor win a great race in the flesh, but first there would be three more disappointments.

Sir Ivor did not have the bug, but it was felt that the Epsom Derby had drained him for a while. Piggott's contention that he was not a true stayer had been clearly confirmed. Sir Ivor lost his next three races, going down in the Eclipse Stakes at Sandown and, in the space of a week, the Prix Henri Delamarre and the Arc de Triomphe. He was not disgraced, yielding to the superb Vaguely Noble in the Arc, and he burst back in Newmarket's Champion Stakes. He would not tackle the mile and three quarters of the St Leger. His last race would be the Washington International at Laurel.

Piggott was to ride him then but before that he would go to Town Moor, Doncaster. He would attempt to win his fourth St Leger. Fulke Johnson Houghton's consolation prize had responded well to the glory of The Curragh. Ribero was in fine condition. He looked even stronger than he had in Ireland. There was just one problem: he had a mouth abscess.

A mouth abscess in a racehorse is rather like faulty

handling in a Grand Prix car. It places immense responsibility on the man who has to steer. Fulke Johnson Houghton recalls:

> If Piggott hadn't been up one would have been terribly depressed about our chances – even with Piggott up it was frustrating and very worrying. It meant Lester couldn't hedge Ribero for a second. He had to ride a perfectly balanced race. His options were so limited. It would take a kind of ultimate skill. One suspected Lester had it, of course.

Rain swept across the Town Moor course. The going was soft, and this was something to balance the problem of Ribero's abscess. Connaught, who so dramatically put Ribero to the sword at Ascot, detested soft going. Noel Murless wore his bleakest expression. 'This won't suit Connaught at all,' he said, 'he's all at sea in soft going.'

Murless's fears were confirmed half-way up the long straight. Sandy Barclay had kept him close up on the leaders, Cold Storage and Alignment, up to the final turn, but could not prevent Connaught from floundering. Piggott, who had not forgotten for a second Ribero's painfully ulcerated lip, was perfectly placed. At his first urging Ribero accelerated powerfully into the lead. There was just one threat. Bill Williamson had nursed Canterbury into a powerful run. Canterbury had been struggling coming into the straight, so badly in fact that Williamson had been tempted to pull him up. Alignment was hanging on, but it was clear one and a half furlongs out that the issue was between Ribero and Canterbury, who was inching close to the lead with every stride. The roars of the Yorkshire crowd wafted across the great misty expanse of Town Moor. So many times in the past Piggott had generated immense power. So many times it had pulled him through by the barest margin. Here his great strength was neutralized. If he was to win he had to sit it out. He had to be still, utterly composed, as he knew that one false ounce of pressure would be disastrous.

Williamson's easy, gentle touch was drawing a great dividend. It seemed that he had picked off Piggott. They went to the line together and in the wait for the photo finish the bookmakers clearly believed that this time the Long Fella had gone down. Piggott himself had no such misapprehension. His face did not betray emotion. He simply headed for the winners' enclosure. Later, he said, 'I knew he had won – and I knew he was putting it all in. That's why I didn't touch him.' He smiled when he said that, and years later Fulke Johnson Houghton confirmed:

We know that Lester is always reluctant to show his true feelings, but I sensed that day at Doncaster that he was very pleased with himself. I knew what he had done – and he knew what had been done. It was a simply brilliant piece of riding. There had been so much touch, so much feel. I can't imagine that anyone has ever ridden a better race. Really, the fellow defies the imagination.

In a long and revealing interview with Kenneth Harris of *The Observer* Piggott gave a clue to his winning combination of power and touch.

A jockey has got to make horses want to run for him. Sometimes a horse and a jockey won't hit it off. Then, you've got to have judgement – can you get through the gap or not? Is the pace too slow? Is it so slow that if I poach a lead of four lengths here, three furlongs out, I can hang on and win by a neck? And you've got to do your homework – find out as much as you can about the other horses, so that when you see one in front of you, you can guess what he can do. Sometimes you can work out tactics in advance, but sometimes you've got to change them. Sometimes they don't come off. You've got to keep thinking about racing all the time – it's no good starting to think about a race just before you get up on the horse's back. That's one thing about not wanting to talk very much – I get time to read about racing, and to listen, and to think.

It might be the working pattern of a great philosopher, but then Piggott is one of the few men who have really come to terms with the nature of their lives. It wasn't all learning that enabled him to bring off his astonishing triumph on Ribero, it was the life he had lived.

14 Taking on the World

Up in the press gallery of Laurel Park, Washington DC, the American racing journalists chewed their cigar stubs, rubbed their eyes, shook their heads, and exchanged some Anglo-Saxon expletives. The whole procedure was the preliminary ritual to an attack on a professional sportsman virtually unprecedented in a society where the freedom of the press is a fact of life. The object of their scorn was Lester Piggott. In the sober columns of such papers as *The New York Times* and *Washington Post* long, theoretical pieces appeared, all effectively saying the same thing: Lester Piggott was a 'limey bum'! This was the extraordinary climax to 1968 when Piggott took Sir Ivor out for his last race.

The Americans knew about Piggott. They had seen him ride and wondered about his European reputation. They were confused by his waiting style, his tendency to delay the final move to the last furlong. In America the race rider worked more to the pace of the race, seeking to grind down the opposition with the superiority of his horse. The Americans thought Lester Piggott didn't know about pace! They thought his reputation 'soft' and when they saw his manœuvre on the back stretch of the 1968 Washington International they said that here was the final proof that the limey couldn't live with men like Willie 'the Shoe' Shoemaker, Braulio Baeza and the hook-nosed Eddie Arcaro. Certainly Piggott performed an interesting switch of tactics half-way through the race. He seemed to be trapped on the rails, sixth of eight runners, when he suddenly checked Sir Ivor, went last, and swung to the outside. The gasps in the press gallery were reproduced around the track. The pacemakers were the American fancies, Czar Alexander (Jorge Velasquez), Fort Marcy (Manuel Ycaza), and a Japanese contender, Takeshiba-O. The big French colt Carmarthen also looked menacing.

'The limey has blown it,' said the Americans who knew. But they didn't know Piggott or his understanding of the animal he rode. They didn't know what he knew about Sir Ivor's capacity, when, perfectly gathered, he released a burst of speed which simply ate up the ground. And this was soft ground. Piggott had to conserve the speed. What he needed was a glimpse of daylight and within a hundred yards of his startling move he had found it. To exploit it he had to show patience. Of all the qualities that Piggott had inherited and developed, patience – at least in riding a race – may be the most striking. In the straight Czar Alexander and Fort Marcy continued their duel, Velasquez and Ycaza working furiously.

A furlong out the Americans seemed certain to have it. Then Piggott thrust Sir Ivor through a gap and in the last strides Epsom in June was gloriously re-created. It was all there again, the surge of speed, the perfect balance, the blending of man and horse. The Americans rubbed their eyes again. But they didn't throw up their arms to salute the limey bum. As far as they were concerned he had made a good horse look bad, and their feelings were made clear in the press conference afterwards. Piggott was appalled and angry. The questions all followed the same theme. Why had he been so slow to move, putting Sir Ivor's chances at risk? Piggott snapped angrily at one pressman, 'Get out of here!' He might have added that justifying himself had never been one of his favourite chores, even to men of the calibre of Noel Murless and Vincent O'Brien. He strode out of the press room. Later, he could look back calmly on the American press's comments.

They said some stupid things, but then I suppose they have a job to do and I'm not too worried about how they do it. When you have been doing the same thing for twenty years you ride along with the praise and the criticism. I have won by a short head after making a hell of a mess of things earlier and then read of my brilliance. At other times I have done everything right, just got done on the post, and read that I made a hash of everything. But I get annoyed when people delve too much into theory, when they try to tell you what you should have done. There is only one place to be making decisions – that's out on the back of the horse. I know mistakes happen; sometimes you can get it wrong, of course. But if you have enough experience, if you have thought about the race, I really think you are the best judge of what needs doing. They slammed me after I won with Sir Ivor in Washington, but I just couldn't accept their criticism. I didn't think they were qualified to make any judgements. I knew a bit more about Sir Ivor than they did. I also knew the going was very soft. I knew what I had to do.

Raymond Guest has no reservations. He had watched agonizingly from the stand with his big-shot Washington friends, the politicians and diplomats, and in those last yards of the Laurel straight his passion for horse-racing had come to a magnificent climax. Piggott, mud-spattered, took hold of the trophy and gave one of his rare smiles. It seemed to come up from his boots and showed deep satisfaction.

When reviewing 1968 it is not hard to understand Piggott's feelings that soggy day in Washington DC. The criticism of the American press was only weak shot fired by men out of range of his experience. On Sir Ivor and Ribero he had brought further definition to the title of master jockey. He was not without some admirers at Washington, the most impressive being Clive Graham, who for many years shared with Peter O'Sullevan a partnership of brilliant distinction for both the *Daily Express* and the BBC. Graham offered the opinion that this was Piggott's finest hour. Perhaps he was goaded into saying this by the fierce reactions of his American colleagues, but Graham is well known for his clear racing judgement. If he said Piggott's Washington ride was his best to date, then we can be sure it was a superb piece of riding.

Piggott, as he stood beside the waters of the Potomac, knew that his point had been made more spectacularly than anyone could ever have imagined. 1967 had been a year of snatched achievement, prizes gleaned from under great pressure; 1968 had been more of a parade. The American criticism unquestionably rankled deeply because it came at the end of a run of performances which removed any misgivings against his talent. His mood was captured by a glancing reference he made of one American reporter: 'He looked as if he would fall off a horse – if he ever got near one.'

Years later Piggott's affection for Sir Ivor burned just as brightly as in those days at Newmarket, Epsom and Washington. He always said Sir Ivor was his favourite.

He was a little bit headstrong but marvellous to ride because he just liked to get on with the job. And he had that terrific turn of foot. He was able to produce it even though the Derby was just a bit long for him. He must be one of the best Derby winners ever.

Piggott had a consuming taste for the classics now: Newmarket in the spring, Epsom in June and the autumn climax at Doncaster. The Jockey's Championship had become a fact of his life, although he was beginning to weary of its demands.

It's true that you must come to a point when you want to be more selective I'm far from being tired of it all. The big races, the classics, well they do so much for you, get the blood going. But sometimes it is hard, following an afternoon's racing, to have to drag yourself to an evening meeting – I'm not happy about evening racing.

It became clear over those years when he had clearly established himself as the world's great jockey, that there was much about his life which did not always appeal to him.

Sometimes you get the idea that you are living in a goldfish bowl, and it does get depressing. This is not a sport to be big-headed in. If I sometimes appear that way it is because things that are commonplace with me strike other people as unusual. There are some who think that in the middle of a busy afternoon they have every right to stick a microphone in front of me and discuss some vital issue or what I had for breakfast. I'm often asked how I feel about riding a horse when huge sums are involved and a mistake will wreck everything. To do this job properly you must feel the same way every time. A captain of a ship doesn't spend his life at sea worrying about the cost of the boat. He is too busy doing things right. It irritates me when I sense people hovering around, latching on to everything I say ... maybe in the paddock before a race. Some people imagine that every time I talk it's on some matter of life or death. There have been fellows who station themselves opposite me in an attempt to do a bit of lip-reading. They have been perhaps shocked when they found me discussing the price of a share or the picture Susan and I went to the night before.

Racing is glamorous to a lot of people. The huge sums involved have a lot to do with this. But there is no glamour for the jockey – just a lot of damned hard work. I have probably done a day's work before I get to the races. There are times when it would be nice to forget it for a week.

We all have those times when it is hell to get out of bed and follow the same routine. It's at these times even the quietest of jockeys blow their tops. If I weren't able to cut myself off from the nonsense and this business of being a celebrity I would not last a season. The only things that have shaken me have been the warnings and fines and suspensions. The sport is dangerous but you would never make it if you thought of the danger. Great jockeys like Manny Mercer have been killed and others put off the sport but as in motor racing it would not do to dwell on these things. Scobie Breasley is the most marvellous old character. In spite of all the crashes, he went on racing well into his fifties. I don't think I'll go on as long as that. Maybe another ten years.

Piggott said that rather more than ten years ago, and though retirement is now on the horizon it could still take a few more years.

The switch from Murless to freelancing, from the steady job with superb fringe benefits to the open market of privateering, was mainly prompted by ambition, but Piggott was also reacting to the drudgery required in winning the Jockeys' Championship. Ironically, the switch threw a new weight of work on him. He sat at the fine desk bought by his wife and he absorbed form as a mathematician might swallow whole theorems. He always wanted to be poised to strike for the rich booty, the good thing.

The young trainer, Philip Mitchell, described Piggott as a fascinating case.

His brain, its capacity, is astonishing. You watch him in a race in which he realizes his own horse has no chance. His head will be swivelling around, taking in every other animal in the race. He will go back to the locker-room with a whole dossier in his brain. I don't know whether he goes home to Newmarket and writes it all down, or whether it just lodges there on some peculiar index file. The point is that one day you will be amazed to pick up the phone and hear the great Lester Piggott telling you that a horse of yours was unlucky at Folkstone three weeks ago and that he fancies riding it next time out.

Lester is tough and ruthless, of course, but before you make any criticism of him you first have to say that there is nobody like him in the whole world of racing. He's a complete one-off.

Inevitably the self-imposed pace of his life led to mishaps and spectacular flashes of tension and for every incident, however trivial, there was a vast audience. There was a scene at Washington Airport where British Airways officials refused him his seat. There was trouble over a boarding card. Piggott was said to be 'difficult'. The Jockey Club Stewards once fined him £100 and cautioned him for his attitude towards a vet. The vet had reported Piggott for 'excessive use of the whip' after he had ridden a 6–5 favourite into third place. The vet, course official Alastair Limont, and Piggott appeared before the stewards and were dismissed. Piggott was then alleged to have made a remark to Limont which was something other than, 'Have a nice day, Alastair, old chap'.

Piggott was often told that as a senior jockey he should watch his behaviour on a racecourse. Before his St Leger triumph on Ribero he was subject to violent threats during the September meeting at Epsom. Local police received a curt message: 'An attempt will be made on Lester Piggott's life this afternoon.' Police and security guards combed the course. There was a certain tension in the air but it was undetected by Piggott. He rode three winners.

In the early sixties Piggott began to commute regularly to Paris on Sundays, usually staying at the Hôtel Claridge in the Champs Elysées which has a good Turkish bath. One Sunday he fell foul of the customs men checking on currency and this led to a court appearance. His defence counsel claimed: 'He is in a position to demonstrate for Britain the supremacy of our riding, the leadership of British bloodstock, and the determination to compete and win.' Piggott's 'crime' was to ignore the £65 travelling allowance.

Piggott easily grew resentful at petty officialdom, whether at airports, racecourses or radar speed-traps.

He also resented suggestions that he was a millionaire and usually had a ready retort.

It is ridiculous to say I'm worth a million. I pay taxes like everyone else, but I'm pretty well off because I don't chuck money around. When you make the sacrifices I do, drive yourself for most of the year as I do, you value the stuff. In my case there is always the strain of dieting. I've kept down to 8 st 5 lb for the last ten years, but I have to work at it. I can never eat lunch and I really have to forget about having a drink. I'm not complaining about this. It is my life, what I've decided to do. But I don't like people giving the impression that I'm making lots of easy money. I work for what I get.

Piggott's chauffeur earned his money on a relentless criss-cross of the English tracks, gunning the big new Mercedes from afternoon to evening meetings. Sometimes, when Piggott had to make the weight in quick time he discarded the chauffeur, on humanitarian grounds, put on a rubber suit and drove away, windows closed and heater full blast. And no lunch. Sometimes his chauffeur felt the generous side of Piggott, normally only revealed to family and close friends.

One Saturday night he rang me up and said he was whacked. He asked me to drive him to London Airport on the Sunday morning for the plane to Paris. He told me to bring the wife and kids. When we got to Heathrow he gave me £15 to take the family out to lunch at Windsor. Really, he's a wonderful boss.

There can be no question that he would drive anyone harder than himself.

By the winter of 1968 Piggott had reason to reflect on the rigours of his life, and it was reasonable that on the flight home from the Washington International triumph he should begin to think of withdrawing from the annual hard labour of pursuing the championship. He had already won it six times. There was nothing to prove on the long course now, he had won it out on his own and had also proved that there could be vast rewards for a man who set himself up for the big races. In that respect 1969 looked a very good year indeed.

In the autumn he had ridden the two-year-old brother of his great allies, Ribocco and Ribero, Ribofilio. The latest son of Ribot looked as though he had been custom-built for Lester Piggott. He was quick and strong and he flew in for the Dewhurst Stakes. But Ribofilio was a maker of illusions. He looked superior to his opposition, but throughout his bewildering career he kept intact his reputation as a prodigal son. In 1969 he was made favourite for the Two Thousand Guineas, the Derby, the Irish Derby, and the St Leger. Each time he failed, and each time Lester Piggott winced. For once it seemed that the famous antennae were faulty.

Even more surprisingly, he spurned the old device of cutting his losses. Geoff Lewis, the bell-boy whose ambitions to race had been triggered by reading about Piggott's youthful exploits, had brought home his first English classic winner, a 15–2 shot, Right Tack, trained by Piggott's friend, John Sutcliffe. Lewis, who was also challenging Piggott's hold of the championship, might have hoped for a more glorious entry into the classic lists. Most of the eyes which raked the Rowley Mile centred on Ribofilio, described by his owner Engelhard as 'the last of the cheap Ribots'. Piggott reported after the race that Ribofilio, had showed such lack of life that he could 'scarcely raise a gallop'. At one stage the stunned crowd imagined Piggott was about to pull up. Fulke Johnson Houghton and Piggott conferred forlornly; the stewards ordered a dope test. It was negative.

Before the 1969 Derby, which had failed to produce anything like a hard favourite, or even impressive contenders, Johnson Houghton gave Ribofilio a spin at Sandown – and was encouraged. Piggott kept his faith in the colt, perhaps seduced by the tenacity of Ribocco and Ribero, and surprisingly enough Ribofilio was favourite at the dawn of the

Derby. Briefly, after Tattenham Corner, Piggott produced Ribofilio for a run which hinted at menace, but the cries of his backers were almost instantly cut off. Ernie Johnson, a jockey so light that some said he would never get a serious classic hope, smoothly brought in Blakeney. We can be certain that the fact Johnson had spent much of his Epsom preparation studying films of Piggott's triumphs on Never Say Die, Crepello, St Paddy, and Sir Ivor did little to mollify the great man. In the Irish Derby Ribofilio's form had improved to the extent that he seriously challenged the winner, Prince Regent (Geoff Lewis) right up to the last few strides. Again at Doncaster Piggott elected to ride the mysterious Ribofilio, and again he suffered dire frustration, finishing second to Ron Hutchinson on the 7–1 Intermezzo. 'It was a shame about Ribofilio,' said Piggott. 'He was a brilliant two-year-old and there were times when you felt he was just about to come off, but that's the thing about racing. You can be very close – and still a long way away.'

Ribofilio was almost a reassurance that the game had not come completely to the heel of Lester Piggott; that in the end its whims and caprices were beyond the calculations of a mind as sharply analytical as his. But if the 1969 classic season was a desert to Piggott there was an oasis or two. He won the Eclipse Stakes on Wolver Hollow, beating Geoff Lewis on the brilliant mare, Park Top. Later Lewis confessed that he had ridden a bad race, and added ruefully that of course Piggott chose that day to put in one of his most brilliant performances. 'You could count on that couldn't you?' Piggott took over Park Top and swept her to victory along the rails in the King George VI and Queen Elizabeth Stakes. But 1969 was an elusive year; great prizes came tantalizingly near, then slipped through his fingers. In the Arc de Triomphe he squared up to responsibility for a mistimed challenge on Park Top, losing out to Bill Williamson on the wide sweep of Longchamp. This time Williamson was riding Levmoss. Piggott counter-attacked that very afternoon and four times he brought in winners to the enclosure shaded by chestnut trees.

In the Jockeys' Championship he had worn down the

brave and consistently enterprising Lewis, and would do so for two more years. His fast-growing popularity in France had pushed him towards the decision that he must do more racing abroad. Earlier in the year he had replied to a question about his championship prospects:

I don't really know this time. It might be a good thing for racing if somebody else – Geoff Lewis or Sandy Barclay – took over. I suppose if the race gets interesting I could easily change my mind. I won't set out to win the championship next year. Again, it is something that could just happen,

Geoff Lewis said much the same.

Of course it is something which could just happen – and God knows how long it will keep just happening. Lester is a man you simply can't read. You might think you have him, but you're kidding yourself. He will always come back at you. He's always there. It's as though nothing on earth can stop him when he has set his mind on something.

During the winter of 1968–9 Piggott had had one recurring thought on his mind. He would go back to Washington DC and he would impale those American critics; he would exact a spectacular revenge for their loose words and loose thinking over the Sir Ivor finish. His vehicle would be Karabas, a powerful four-year-old owned by Lord Iveagh and trained by Bernard van Cutsem. Piggott would ridicule the critics, both with his dry, dismissive wit and his racecraft. 11 November 1969 was for America's racing press the Day of Atonement. Piggott had come into town with the swagger of a gunfighter sure of the inferior quality of his challengers. The bookmakers agreed with the press, though, installing the American horse Hawaii as favourite and offering Karabas at 7–2. Everyone who saw him at the course agreed that Piggott's demeanour was unusual. Before he changed for the race he was seen talking freely to English supporters, amazed by hearing light chatter from the lips of the great man.

Karabas was also in good pre-race form. He had been demolishing oats at the rate of 27 lb a day. At exercise he moved beautifully and stable-lads Michael Ryan and George Walker, who had travelled from England, reported that they had never seen the horse in better shape. Lord Iveagh's racing manager, Frank More O'Ferrall, joined Piggott in a walk around the track, Piggott testing the turf from time to time and grunting approval as a hunter might check his traps. O'Ferrall delayed the big question until the end of the one and a half mile circuit. 'Well, Lester, what do you think? Are we in with a chance?' Piggott replied: 'There's nothing to worry about now. I had one worry, the turf, but I'm not worried about that any more. I've never seen it better. Everything is fine. We will win all right.' From Piggott it was more a statement than a prediction. At the start he was quite impervious to the commotion surrounding the Brazilian contender, Sabinus, who put in an ill-tempered display before being blindfolded and backed into the stalls.

Dan Florestan, an entry from Venezuela, set a brisk pace and was followed by the highly-strung Sabinus, Czar Alexander, German candidate Hitchcock, Hawaii, and then Karabas. Piggott had taken him to the rails. He moved easily into stride and going down the back stretch it was clear from the press stand that Karabas was going to be involved in the finish. There was a certain bracing of the nerve against a limey bum coming in. Moving into the stretch, Czar Alexander and Hawaii had gone beyond the tiring Don Florestan and these two fought for the lead coming off the bend. In their dispute they left room on the rails. Piggott was moving through the gap almost before it had been created. His instinct had been honed to a razor's edge, each insult he had received from the American press serving as a sharpening stroke. There was a note of unanswerable authority in Karabas's move to the lead. The horse had been trained to perfection and a lot of preparation had gone into the rider's performance. Together they left Hawaii and Czar Alexander to fight out the minor prizes, Karabas coming in a length and a quarter in front of Hawaii with Czar Alexander a half length away in third place.

Piggott had never before – or after – been so obviously

delighted by a result. He may have been deeply satisfied by the horsemanship and virtuosity, but this sensation he had before the front ranks of American society was something raw and basic. It was something he felt in his guts. The Americans had been saying such unbelievable things. One writer had said that Piggott was a myth, an eight-pound handicap to a horse.

He was beaming as he brought in Karabas but when an American radio man thrust a microphone towards him the smile turned to ice. His after-race press conference seethed with tension. He recalled his attitude to the press the previous year. 'I told them to get the hell out of the room. Some of them looked as though they would collapse if they took just a couple of minutes in the fresh air.'

One reporter gamely asked: 'When did you think you had the race won, Lester?'

The answer fired back immediately, 'Two weeks ago.' It wasn't meant as a joke. It was a declaration of his own style, a neat bringing together of the great forces of his career: uncanny judgement and relentless confidence. Bernard van Cutsem was giving a less frigid press conference. But his words might have been aimed at the professional hearts of the men who had so violently dismissed the talent of Lester Piggott. To the English writers present, the speech was a familiar one. They had heard it so many times from men like Joe Lawson, Noel Murless, Vincent O'Brien, and Paddy Prendergast. 'Karabas was beautifully ridden,' said van Cutsem. 'The race went as I wanted as far as you can ever plan it. He is a good and charming horse. Lester Piggott? Well, Lester Piggott is Lester Piggott, isn't he? Of course, the man is a master.'

The hiccup of Longchamp earlier that summer had been impressively ejected from his system together with the recurring heartburn of Ribofilio. Another campaign had been rounded beautifully. He flew back to England a contented man. Sir Ivor's criticism had penetrated Piggott's guard more truly than any event since his long suspension in 1954. There is no question that he would have worried the Washington problem until he had come up with the perfect rebuttal. He was pleased that it had come so quickly, so cleanly. He could turn his mind again to more usual priorities.

He could think of the best two-year-olds for 1970 and the prospects for the Two Thousand Guineas and the English Derby. It had been a promising autumn, as hopeful as the one that had preceded the year of Sir Ivor. He had two fancies. There was a French contender called Breton. And there was Nijinsky.

15 The Classic Winner

Vincent O'Brien was at the Woodbine bloodstock sales in Toronto on other business, and it is not unusual for businessman thousands of miles from home to fall in love. O'Brien had what Sicilians call the 'thunderbolt', a flash of instant attraction. The usual context is boy and girl. O'Brien fell for a yearling colt. He was in Toronto to check out a Ribot colt, but the moment he saw Nijinsky he forgot all about the Ribot colt who had anyway not impressed him. 'Well, obviously he looked superb,' recalled O'Brien years later. 'He was beautifully made and had a fine head. But sometimes there is something indefinable about the appeal of a horse. Nijinsky had something indefinable.' O'Brien had a little difficulty in talking Charles Engelhard into parting with $84,000 for the colt. No one had so far paid so much for a Canadian yearling, but Canada had never produced a yearling quite like Nijinsky. Nor was the huge, good-natured and vastly rich Engelhard a man to shy away from high quality. The colt, bred by the shrewd and imaginative Eddie Taylor, would soon define his talent.

It came on to the Tipperary gallops like a March wind, gusting and turbulent but full of the promise of summer. There was some arrogance in the big bay. He tended to look down on his stable colleagues which, in the case of O'Brien's establishment, meant that he was being uppity with the uppity. Nijinsky's family tree had branches of pure excellence. He was by Northern Dancer, who was by Nearctic, who was by Nearco. Northern Dancer had brilliantly challenged America's Triple Crown in 1964, carrying off the Kentucky

Derby and Preakness Stakes before finishing third in the Belmont Stakes.

If Nijinsky behaved exuberantly on the gallops and showed a haughty temperament, it was something O'Brien felt he could tolerate. He sensed freakish talent in the colt.

Vincent O'Brien's intuition first proved its worth on 12 July 1969. Nijinsky's work on the gallops, his thrilling rhythm, the easy surge of speed, had found its way on to the bush telegraph and when he made his début at The Curragh the bookies already had their guards up. Nijinsky was 4–11 in the Erne Maiden Stakes, a six-furlong test. There was no puff of smoke and a flash of lightning. Nijinsky got the result by half a length. It was a solid start. O'Brien brought Nijinsky back to The Curragh three times that summer. Each time he was ridden by Liam Ward, and each time he showed his talent was developing under the pressure of racing. He won all three races and the last of them, the Beresford Stakes, provided the first early test of his willingness to fight. Decies, who was to win the 1970 Irish Two Thousand Guineas, battled well before Nijinsky slipped into overdrive. Ward's report to O'Brien could scarcely have been more encouraging. The colt had relished the scrap.

Piggott had been to Cashel and though he was taciturn about his findings, he liked the look and the feel of the colt. They came together at Newmarket for the Dewhurst Stakes. O'Brien would be able to weigh the potential of Nijinsky and Piggott for the classics. It was pleasant work on an October afternoon. O'Brien's decision to move from National Hunt to the flat had been as dramatically successful as Piggott's break from Warren Place. Now both men could be seen clearly in their new spheres. They were ruthless raiders of opportunity and in the Dewhurst the racing fraternity discovered that once again the Piggott–O'Brien axis was tightening a grip on some of the game's richest booty. The margin of victory was a comfortable three lengths, but on the day it was more devastating than that. Piggott kept Nijinsky covered until a furlong and a half out, then smoothly increased the pace. Nijinsky cruised away from his challengers Recalled and Sandal. There had been no dramatic evidence of speed, nor had it been asked for. Both colt and jockey looked as if their only threat had been a sudden onset of boredom. Piggott abandoned thoughts of riding the French horse Breton.

Nijinsky went against four-year-olds at The Curragh the following March, carrying the Gladness Stakes by four lengths. Ward had claimed his Irish rights for this race. But it would be Piggott and Nijinsky for the 1970 Two Thousand Guineas. The compatibility factor was enormous. Both man and horse knew how good they were. There would be no tension or uncertainty in either. The Two Thousand Guineas threw up only one serious challenger, Yellow God, but despite the fine, rhythmic work of Bill Williamson, Piggott had only to hint at the need for extra power and Nijinsky drew away, a winner by two and a half lengths.

Some critics were sceptical about Nijinsky's ability to stay the Derby course, suggesting, as they had with Sir Ivor, that one and a half miles would explore too thoroughly a pedigree which leaned towards sprinting. William Hill was among the sceptics, but if O'Brien shared this concern – and behind his impassive expression his emotions can run from ecstasy to torment without the vaguest threat of detection – he must have been soothed by Piggott's clipped report, which was simply, 'He had plenty left.'

It had been effortless work and Nijinsky was installed at 11–8 favourite. Scepticism is one thing. Lunatic avoidance of all the available facts is something which bookmakers, least of all William Hill, do not practise seriously. Gyr, another North American bred contender, trained in France by the ageing Etienne Pollet, was considered the most potent challenge to Nijinsky. The doubt about Gyr was not stamina – he was by Sea Bird – but sureness of foot on the run down to Tattenham Corner. Gyr was big, leggy, volatile – all qualities which made him vulnerable on the descent which Willie Shoemaker had described as a 'ski slope'. Gyr was rated at 100–30. The only other serious support was for Approval, an Alcide colt which caused some heads to turn in the paddock, and Stintino, a French prospect which had carried the Prix Lupin. Bill Williamson was on Gyr, Gerard

Thiboeuf on Stintino, Greville Starkey on Approval, and almost every housewife in England was on Piggott and Nijinsky. The bookies stood to lose more than £2 million. We can only speculate on how fervently they fanned the flame of scepticism about Nijinsky's staying power. Certainly, they found little encouragement in the paddock beyond the sleek lines of Approval. Nijinsky and Piggott joined the great Derby parade before the stand in the manner of virtuosi awaiting the flourish of the baton.

There was no way of telling that only a few days earlier Piggott had collapsed at Newmarket after straying over the barrier between effective wasting and a sweeping onslaught on the human frame. He had restored himself, achieved again the strange and lonely equilibrium of his professional life. He had made it to the foothills of his fifth Derby victory and at the start there was a hopeful sign.

Gyr, the erratic but dangerous contender, was giving Bill Williamson a difficult time getting into the start stall. Long Till (Duncan Keith) and Cry Baby (Sandy Barclay) took the field away at a brisk pace. By Tattenham Corner the worst fears of Gyr's supporters were proved groundless. Gyr, beautifully coaxed by the soft touch of Williamson, had flowed down the hill and held a strong fifth position. Trainer Pollet's decision to delay his retirement until after Gyr's three-year-old career suddenly seemed like a profitable move. Of the early leaders all fell away except the surprisingly tenacious Great Wall, an 80–1 shot who was being given every chance of glory by the immaculate Joe Mercer. For seconds it seemed that Piggott, astonishingly, might be trapped. Two furlongs out Gyr took it up from Great Wall, and thousands of binoculars raked the straight for Nijinsky. He was coming. Piggott had moved him out effortlessly. The power of the colt was wonderful to see. It rippled through every limb and in a few seconds the hopes of Etienne Pollet had been brushed aside. Nijinsky eased away from Gyr, coming in by two and a half lengths. Stintino fought clear of Great Wall for third place. The winning time was 2 mins 34.6 secs; the fastest since Charlie Smirke had blazed home on Mahmoud in 1936 with a time 2 mins 33.8 secs. Piggott, still subdued from his bad wasting experience, was expressionless as he brought the great colt into the winners' enclosure. He would brighten later when he learned of Engelhard's gratitude, his swift payment of a 'very generous' present and his opinion, 'There is no way I want to see Lester Piggott and Nijinsky apart. They make a wonderful couple.'

It is extraordinary to think how many times rich men had come to see this scrawny, withdrawn figure as a kind of guardian of their most vivid hopes. First there was old Robert Sterling Clark, day-dreaming in his New York nursing-home; the intense and complex plutocrat Sir Victor Sassoon; the amiable Raymond Guest. Now it was Engelhard, the huge chairman of Engelhard Minerals and Chemicals Corporation. Piggott had given him many successes on the brothers Ribocco and Ribero, but this boiling day at Epsom was the pay-off for a huge investment. Engelhard had spent millions of dollars in pursuit of the great prizes of racing. He had 125 horses in training in America, Ireland, England, and France, and 260 bloodstock animals. As he leant on his stick in the winners' enclosure he said, 'This is the happiest day of my life.' It was a fast dwindling life. He would be dead inside the year, and possibly his emotion had something to do with the knowledge or at least a suspicion of this. He declared:

I've wanted to win this race for twenty-two years, and now I know I was right to want it so badly. Nijinsky is a wonderful animal. Lester Piggott is a wonderful jockey, and Vincent O'Brien is a master of training. This is all too marvellous. I also met the Queen!

Engelhard was usually so tense during a big race that he couldn't bring himself to follow the progress of his contender. He preferred to look at the facial expressions of his racing manager, David McCall. Now Engelhard had caught the public fever generated by his colt. The stride was so imperious, the rhythm so moving in its perfection.

I must admit I started off looking down and glancing at David's expression. Then I felt the excitement pouring through me and I saw David was smiling, confident. I just got drawn into it. I watched every stride of it down the last two furlongs. I would be kicking myself now if I had not done so. How many times does a Nijinsky come into your life ... and how many times can you hope to see your colt going for victory in the Derby? I'm not sure how much money I put on Nijinsky. I guess it was around a thousand pounds.

I put the money on to buy the lads some drinks. The prize money [£63,000] will soon be eaten up. If you have a few hundred horses to feed each day you can soon get rid of it. Boy, there are going to be an awful lot of happy horses around tonight.

There was also a very happy breeder. Eddie Taylor had flown in for the Derby. Graciously, Engelhard had passed him the leading rein and invited him to take a lap of honour around the winners' enclosure. Taylor had accepted, muttering: 'Great, wonderful . . . what a colt!' It is not hard to appreciate the special satisfaction of the breeder. However well a jockey rides, a trainer trains, and an owner buys, they are dependent on the quality of raw material which comes into their hands. Nijinsky represented a perfect example of the breeder's art. It is true that Nijinsky had a less than perfect nature, but who argues with a touch of arrogance in a genuine star? Certainly not Mme Romola Nijinsky, widow of the superb Russian dancer; she had instructed her secretary to back the horse named for her husband each time out. Rarely can sentiment have yielded such a hard return.

Though Engelhard had made a strong point about his belief in the unique combination of Piggott and Nijinsky, O'Brien's arrangement with Liam Ward was unshakeable. It was the Irishman who partnered Nijinsky when he returned to The Curragh for the Irish Sweeps Derby. The Guinness and the whiskey flowed even more generously than usual on the eve of Ireland's great race. Two years earlier it had been Sir Ivor striding into the mists of Irish legend, and, so quickly, came another horse to revere and extol and, quite simply, drink to as long as the money and the legs held out. The Irish Derby of 1970 was not so much a race as a coronation. Piggott elected to ride Meadowville, and rode him well.

It would have been impossible to reproduce the extraordinary eye for opportunity which had given him the Irish Sweeps Derby win over Sir Ivor in 1968. Nijinsky eased home by three lengths. Piggott rode a perfect race on Meadowville, but it was simply a question of class; Meadowville had come up against another, higher level of achievement.

On the road home to Dublin, and in all the throbbing hostelries that Saturday night, it took a brave man to say that Nijinsky had something to prove. But there is a catch to winning the Two Thousand Guineas and the Derby. There are always questions about the opposition, about whether the year's crop of three-year-olds is good, bad or indifferent. There was no question about Nijinsky's class, but how would he perform when really tested? As Nijinsky was being spoken of as the potential 'horse of the century' the theorists were anxious to see him against formidable opposition.

The opportunity came soon enough in the King George VI and Queen Elizabeth Stakes. Nijinsky had Piggott back and the feeling was that he would need him. The challenge to Nijinsky's hundred per cent record in eight races came chiefly from the 1969 Derby winner Blakeney, French Oaks winner Crepellana, Piggott's Washington partner Karabas, and the Coronation Cup winner Caliban. As it turned out it was scarcely a contest. Piggott was in control of the race throughout, easing up at the post, two lengths clear of the well-stretched Blakeney. For Engelhard the Royal Ascot victory was another thrill, but also a sharpening of his dilemma about the future of Nijinsky. He was obsessed with the quality of Ribot, mainly because of the great horse's unbeaten record. He wanted the same mystical strength of reputation for his Nijinsky. If Nijinsky carried the St Leger it would be the first Triple Crown since Freddy Fox guided in the Aga Khan's Bahram. Both O'Brien and Piggott believed that the Doncaster classic lay at their mercy. And so, of course, it did.

When Piggott went down to the Leger start he was in a sour mood, which says much for his temperament. Some of his rivals would have been close to hysteria. First, he had been beaten by a short head on a 7–4 on shot, a development which he invariably finds about as amusing as fierce toothache. In the next race he was riding a horse called Leander but, as it turned out, not for long. Leander came lurching out of the stall in a fashion which would have gone down rather better at Denver than Doncaster on St Leger Day. Leander made a series of bizarre jumps, finally sending Piggott crashing to the turf. Piggott marched back to the jockeys' room quite wordlessly. Piggott being thrown from a horse in public not only startles but offends the senses. In any event, Piggott was cross. And Nijinsky? He was also afflicted. He had been badly affected by ringworm since his superb gallop through the high summer, and his preparation for the Leger had been sketchy, at least by the standards of Vincent O'Brien. His coat was not so lustrous as it had been at Newmarket, Epsom, The Curragh, and Ascot, one flank having moulted. Piggott later said: 'That summer he was as good a horse as there has been around since the war, but when he came back in the autumn he wasn't the same.' He was still utterly superior to the rest of the St Leger field.

Johnny Seagrave on Meadowville, and Sandy Barclay on Charlton, made a formal attempt to test Nijinsky's stamina and coming into the straight they entertained hopes of holding on to their advantage. Piggott had been idling Nijinsky at the rear of the field.

Seagrave and Barclay might have been throwing pebbles at the moon. Piggott eased Nijinsky beyond them over the last two furlongs. The distance was a length and half a length. The Triple Crown had been collected in a canter. History insists that Nijinsky should have left the racecourse for the last time that September afternoon. He had been syndicated for £2,266,666, and would join Sir Ivor at the great stud farm Claiborne, in Kentucky.

But first he would race in the Arc and, after that disaster, he would be given the chance to redeem himself over a mile and a quarter at Newmarket in the Champion Stakes. Piggott was pilloried for his Arc performance. He was accused of the old arrogance, of asking too much of Nijinsky's final surge. Piggott claimed that the high draw had affected his options severely but still insisted that it had simply gone wrong in the last two furlongs. The French Derby winner Sassafras beat Nijinsky by a head, Yves St Martin riding a powerful finish. O'Brien, disconsolate, did not argue with suggestions that Piggott had given Nijinsky too much to do

... and after the disappointments with Sir Ivor and Park Top at Longchamp it was a heavy blow to the Long Fella. However, Roger Mortimer makes a good case for Piggott.

> Piggott was sharply criticized on the grounds that he left Nijinsky with far too much to do. The film of the race, though, showed that Nijinsky was nicely placed and was not more than three lengths behind Sassafras when he made his challenge. A hundred and fifty yards from home he was level with Sassafras and would undoubtedly have won had he maintained his run, but he faltered and in the last few strides veered to the left as Piggott wielded the whip with his right hand.

When Troy, the wonder horse of 1979, failed in a similar fashion at Longchamp, no one sought to hammer Willie Carson. The feeling was that Troy had simply run out of steam against the specially-prepared filly, Three Troikas. Nijinsky, apart from possible fatigue, had the additional problem of ringworm. It is also true that horses, like men, can tire of the old routine. They wonder, when the boss snaps out an order, why is this so important?

O'Brien took Nijinsky to Newmarket convinced that the ending would be in the winners' enclosure. O'Brien has always been a master of shrewd decision, always keeping his emotions on a tight reign, but it seems reasonable to suspect an emotional base to the journey to headquarters. Certainly it was another painful blow when the five-year-old Lorenzaccio carried the Champion Stakes.

Piggott was able to absorb the blow less painfully than O'Brien. Although he admired Nijinsky, it is clear that he never felt the gut attachment which had gone out to Zucchero, Crepello, Petite Etoile, and Sir Ivor. Nijinsky was O'Brien's creation and passion, and it was natural that he should feel most the ending to the dream that had first been formed in the bloodstock sales at Woodbine, Toronto. Engelhard had wanted Nijinsky to be unbeaten, but it was clear that his last days were still brightly coloured by the sight of his colt moving down the Epsom straight. For Piggott the emotions could scarcely be so isolated. He had spent his life with great horses. Nijinsky was perhaps the greatest, but he had plenty of time left. There would be more great horses.

16 Only the Best Will Do

Obscured somewhat by Nijinsky's first classic win in May 1970, was the fact that Lester Piggott had laid claim to the last, elusive English classic, the One Thousand Guineas. Again there is evidence against the belief that Piggott is impervious to historic moments. He wore a great smile when he brought in Humble Duty in 1970, a beautifully-prepared grey filly which gave Peter Walwyn his first English classic success. Piggott got the ride because Walwyn's stable jockey Duncan Keith had preceded Piggott along the grim route of wasting to the point of ill health. Keith's mood, later buoyed by the arrival of a crate of champagne from Piggott, cannot have been improved by seeing the televised race which made it clear that Humble Duty's win was one of the easiest of the post-war years. The exuberant Piggott said, 'On good ground this is a wonderful filly. Her acceleration was just terrific.' Humble Duty had surged beyond the fancied French contender Gleam the moment Piggott asked for more.

The Humble Duty episode is a good example of the benefits of Piggott's role in racing. He was the trouble-shooter *par excellence*, the man who could come in at a minute's notice and solve the big race worries of a leading trainer; always assuming, that is, the trainer could fight his way to the head of the queue. Piggott could scout out the good rides, watch out for the two-year-old which had the special promise of classic glory. For the rest of his career Lester Piggott would always be poised to take advantage of the ebb and flow of racing fortune. Sometimes Piggott's very freedom of action can lead him to unproductive gambles, and in the matter of making a costly commitment there is no better example than that of Apalachee, a colt which seemed set to dominate 1974 just as profoundly as Nijinsky had controlled the classics of 1970.

Michael Phillips, respected racing correspondent of *The Times*, wrote in the spring of 1974:

Vincent O'Brien holds the strongest hand in Europe this year. If anyone thinks otherwise a visit however brief, to Ballydoyle, his home in County Tipperary, will banish any lingering doubt. Numerically, his string may not be strong but quality more than makes up for quantity. The forty racehorses there all boast pedigrees that would please even Debrett's critical eye; and most of them have ability to match. I went there with an open mind and left convinced that Apalachee will win the Two Thousand Guineas and Derby with Lester Piggott riding. He is an awe-inspiring horse to watch. When I returned home I found on my desk Timeform's *Racehorses of 1973*. Take this summary of Apalachee: 'In terms of make, shape, performance and illustrious parentage, Apalachee had everything one looks for in a prospective classics winner. Nor does his temperament leave anything to be desired. In the Observer Gold Cup he behaved very sensibly and came to win his race as and when his jockey wished. *Racehorses of 1973* concludes its chapter on Apalachee by stating emphatically that he will stay the Derby distance and that, although he is big, he is such an excellent mover that it will be surprising if Epsom's turns and gradients inconvenience him. Quite frankly we can see nothing to stop him from winning both the Two Thousand Guineas and the Derby. We have not seen a horse as promising as this for years. Praise indeed, but is it justified, you may well ask? I believe it is. I saw Apalachee in his box in the evening but, more important, also at exercise the following morning. He is the most exceptional mover I have seen. He floats over the ground almost as if he were moving on air, devouring the ground in long easy strides and absolute economy of effort. His is such a natural, relaxed action he seems to be stroking the ground. If he were a cricketer people would marvel at the ease with which he would stroke the ball through the covers, so utterly captivating is he to watch.

There could only be one reaction to such a piece. It would

be to go to the nearest bookmaker and seek some ante-post betting.

In fact, Apalachee never happened in 1974. And Piggott didn't win a classic. It was a rare stretch of rocky ground but it illustrates nicely enough the high-risk game Piggott elected to play when he parted with Noel Murless in the summer of 1966. And of course there was always a glint of gold for a man capable of riding the sort of finish which carried the small and battling Athens Wood to victory in the 1971 St Leger. In a desperate three-horse finish Piggott got Athens Wood in by a head. Trainer Tom Jones said, 'Lester Piggott is a genius in judging the pace of a race, knowing when to produce a horse for a killing effort.'

The following year at Doncaster Boucher provided Piggott with his seventh, and O'Brien his third, St Leger. Piggott showed a perfect piece of horsemanship on Boucher, easing him through a crisis when he hit soggy going. Three years later Jeremy Tree gave Piggott the choice between two fillies he had trained, Brilliantine and Juliette Marny, for the Oaks. Tree so respected Piggott's judgment he said simply, 'It's up to you,' having decided just three hours before the start that he would run Brilliantine. The feeling had been that Piggott would give the nod to Brilliantine. In the build-up to the race Piggott had said to Tree, 'Come on, which one do you favour?' Tree preferred to leave the choice to Piggott. So many times Piggott had turned a hunch into a fractionally won prize. Juliette Marny was a comfortable winner. She didn't require even a mild reminder. Piggott forced a smile as he unsaddled. Tree, beaming, said, 'Well done, you chose the right one then.'

'Well, I didn't get much help from you,' said Piggott.

Tree's approach seems reasonable. He had produced two likely Oaks contenders and, when he had Lester Piggott available, no man could have passed the responsibility for the choice of winner with an easier conscience.

Throughout the seventies there was recurring evidence of Lester Piggott's capacity to make quick, sure assessments and come away with the spoils. It was also true that if he was denied his favourite, the horse which seemed to fill all the requirements for a race, he could make an excellent job of opting for another candidate which had the equipment to profit from any upset.

In 1976 he, like all the leading jockeys, would have chosen Wollow for the Derby but Wollow's trainer, Henry Cecil, stuck by the Italian rider Franco Dettori, despite the fact that he had never ridden the Derby course before. The French trainer Maurice Zilber pressed the claims of Empery on Piggott, who was highly sceptical about the chances of any colt against Wollow's turn of foot. But he conceded that Empery would make the distance, and there was no such certainty about Wollow. If Piggott could perform his usual ritual, place his mount unerringly through the fast-changing terrain – well, there might be something.

From the spectator's point of view the 1976 Derby had the quintessential quality that draws crowds to the racetrack, the prospect of brave men and horses in pursuit of the supreme prize.

On the eve of the race Piggott said it would take an elephant gun to stop Wollow. He undersold his own talent. Piggott rode so perfectly that Henry Cecil must have been reconsidering his decision even before the final winning strides of Empery. 'Wollow lost his place on the hill,' said Cecil, 'and there was no chance after that.' Jim Shannon, racing manager of Empery's Texan owner, Bunker Hunt, enthused, 'It was just typical Piggott, which is the same as saying magic. We couldn't have had a better man, could we?'

The most stark contrast of all was between Piggott and the grey-faced little Italian, Dettori. Piggott had rarely been so elated. He declared, 'It was bottoms up all the way. I had it from the moment I hit the straight. I feel super. Easily the best moment of my life.' At the same time Dettori was saying, 'This is the worst moment I have known. This wasn't half the horse that won the Guineas. There was no acceleration. The moment we left the box I knew we were in trouble. I feel so bad and depressed I can hardly speak.'

Piggott accepted congratulations from Maurice Zilber and

resurrected his favourite old joke. When asked, 'When did you know you had won?' he would say, 'Last night.'

The Roberto affair is the most controversial instance of Piggott's fierce self-confidence against any amount of opposition. No champion ever had a day of such biting examination as Lester Piggott on 7 June 1972 – Derby Day. He did not merely race against the cream of the year's three-year-olds, contesting with them a racetrack designed to explore every corner of a jockey's talent and resolution; it seemed that when Piggott mounted Roberto he was racing against the world. A born loner, he had ridden to his loneliest position. A quarter of a million people hungry for sensation had come to the downs to see the great Piggott beaten. His popularity was darkened by circumstances over which he claimed, to a cynical if not actually disbelieving audience, he had no control. Piggott had never courted the regard of the public; never been afraid to damn the consequences, and that day at Epsom saw his philosophy reach logical conclusion.

Racing has scarcely known a more emotive story. Eighteen months before the 1972 Derby it seemed that Piggott's vast network of contacts and the computer bank in his own brain would not be required in the selection of a Derby candidate. The colt was already on his own doorstep. It was Crowned Prince, an American-bred colt to be trained by Bernard van Cutsem at Newmarket. Crowned Prince had cost $500,000 as a yearling.

Crowned Prince was beautiful and quick and seemed so powerful there could be no question he would not get Epsom's one and a half mile trip. But the career of Crowned Prince was to be one of those racing stories which sizzles and spurts and then suddenly disappears. He showed immense promise as a two-year-old, winning the Champagne Stakes without a hint of fatigue. Without warning, he ran wretchedly in the Craven Stakes. Van Cutsem was bemused; thinking it over he wondered whether the colt might have a soft palate. He sent Crowned Prince for a trial spin at Yarmouth, bracing himself against the worst. Crowned Prince faulted; he had a soft palate. For van Cutsem twelve months of work and hope was blown away on a bleak afternoon by the sea. Lester Piggott had been heavily committed to Crowned Prince for the Derby. It was not exactly a vintage year, Crowned Prince looking the best of the crop by a wide margin.

Piggott explored form, sent out a score of feelers, but it was an unrewarding search for a substitute. Eventually he turned to his ally Vincent O'Brien, but the best the Irishman could offer was his second string candidate, Manitoulin, a 66–1 shot. O'Brien had the 3–1 favourite Roberto, but Bill Williamson was booked. It was a firm arrangement. Piggott was disconsolate. The Derby had become the centrepiece of his year, the fulcrum of his effort.

Bill Williamson's nickname was 'Weary'. In 1972 he was approaching fifty, dry, wrinkled, and under no illusion about the fact that his career would soon be dwindling away. An Australian, he had won much respect on the racetracks of Britain and Ireland and France. He had wonderful balance and a subtle, almost gentle style; he coaxed rather than domineered. For all its distinction, his career had not yielded a Derby win, the win which overreaches any other professional consideration of the England-based jockey – and Williamson had caught the fever in the spring of 1972. If he didn't win at Epsom now, well, he could consign the Derby to that place where all the broken dreams which accumulate in life go. In a year dramatically denuded by Crowned Prince's absence, Roberto had an excellent chance. It was enough to put spring into Weary's stride.

Roberto was owned by John Galbreath, an archetypal American business tycoon. For him winning was not so much an ambition as an assumption. Galbreath admitted it cheerfully. He was hard – but fair. He owned the Pittsburg Pirates, who had won the World Series in the spring of 1972. Winning the World Series is one of the cornerstones of achievement to an American, something to place in the highest bracket, like winning a Presidential election or the Kentucky Derby. John Galbreath, who was seventy-four, had also won the Kentucky Derby – twice. He had not run for President. Now he had a powerful yearning for the

English Derby. He was silver-haired, sharp-featured, with a vigorous mind and when he made a decision there was no questioning, no second thoughts. When Galbreath sent Roberto to O'Brien he announced: 'I have my eye on some English classics – anyone who doesn't consider the Epsom Derby one of the greatest sports events in the world must be out of his mind. I would love to win it.' He knew he had a good chance with Roberto.

Certainly Roberto had English Derby-winning blood. He was bred by Galbreath at the Darby Dan Farm, Lexington, Kentucky. His relatives included Sir Ivor and Never Say Die, and in his first year in Ireland he looked every bit the young aristocrat. There was a wide blue sky over The Curragh when Roberto made his début. He cruised through the Lagan Maiden Stakes, winning by three lengths. As he drove home through the Vale of Tipperary, the Rock of Cashel standing sentinel in the golden dusk, O'Brien concluded that at the very least he had a contender. All through the summer O'Brien's hopes grew and the messages back to America all spoke of a series of home runs. In August Roberto went back to The Curragh, and delivered a slamming victory in the Anglesey Stakes. This time, in a six-furlong race, he stretched his superiority to six lengths. In September O'Brien presented Roberto with a more searching test, the seven-furlong National Stakes, also at The Curragh. Again Roberto delivered impressively, this time coming in by five lengths.

The Irish were beginning to talk of Roberto as a superhorse. He was compared to Nijinsky, perhaps over-extravagantly, but certainly the Irish strode jauntily along the Champs Elysées when Roberto travelled to Paris in October for the Grand Criterium at Longchamp. Roberto looked well enough in the paddock and the Irish were busy at the Pari-Mutuel betting counters. But Roberto never got to the pace of the race, finishing unplaced behind Hard to Beat, an Irish colt who would pay spectacular interest on his yearling price of 920 guineas.

Had Roberto been doped? There was no statement from the stable. Roberto remained shrouded in mystery throughout the winter. O'Brien and the racing world wondered whether he could stay, whether his appetite for racing had been so quickly satisfied ... O'Brien kept an open mind and did his work. In the spring Roberto came out of Cashel again with much to prove. He travelled to Dublin and on 1 April 1972 he strode through heavy going at Phoenix Park to carry the Vauxhall Trial Stakes. The seagulls were tossed by a wild wind sweeping in from Dublin Bay, but the wet and storm-blown crowd concluded that at least they had seen a colt of considerable substance. He might not be another Nijinsky but he had power and character. The events of the previous autumn in Paris were, if not entirely dismissed, somewhat relegated in importance.

For the Two Thousand Guineas Roberto was installed as second favourite to Sir John Thorn's impressive High Top, a colt who had slaughtered the eventual One Thousand Guineas winner Waterloo. In the Newmarket classic Williamson experienced some difficulty in getting Roberto the sharp pace set by High Top, but after The Bushes Roberto and Williamson did some fine work, pressing High Top all the way to the line. High Top got in by half a length but it would be Roberto who would go to Epsom as Derby favourite. He would not race again before the big day.

For Weary Williamson they were days filled with expectations. He had known all the blows and the pains of racing and he had learned to take them with a phlegmatic shrug. His reputation as a rider of genuine class and judgement had long been secure. What had come to him now was more than the professional regard and respect of every jockey and trainer in the land; all eyes would be directed at him on the racing calendar's greatest day.

It was a wonderful prospect, a late but spectacular reward for all the years of wasting and working, and though a bad fall at Kempton Park ten days before alarmed him, medical examinations brought swift reassurance. If he rested, he would be perfectly fit for the Derby. His body was jarred and painful but there was no damage. He had to nurse the old body for the big one.

Vincent O'Brien, concerned, rang to ask if Williamson

was all right. The Australian was more emphatic than he had been about anything in his life. Nothing, he said, would keep him off the back of Roberto. But something would. Lester Piggott. He and the tough, utterly unsentimental, old American tycoon who said that sport, like life, should be about winning – about making damn sure you give yourself every chance. 'What is the point of competing,' Galbreath asked, 'if you are not prepared to move everything to win?' It seemed that Bill Williamson's hopes were movable objects. Galbreath was not at all happy about the fall at Kempton Park, and the fact that Williamson had been out of the saddle for a week.

If Bill Williamson had to pick out the worst days of his life there is no doubt one would be Monday, 5 June 1972. It was two days before the Derby. The day started well enough. Williamson went to his doctor, Bill Tucker, and submitted to a thorough examination. Naturally he was apprehensive; Bill Williamson was a durable old bird, but fifty is no age to come off the back of a galloping racehorse. He knew he had not long to go as a rider. Tucker's verdict, though, could not have been better. 'You're a hundred per cent fit, Bill,' he said, adding, 'Good luck in the Derby.' Williamson's relief and exhilaration did not last the day. He was summoned to Claridge's Hotel and the opulent suite of John Galbreath. Galbreath, unblinkingly told Williamson that he would not be escorting Roberto around Epsom. Lester Piggott, five times the Derby-winning jockey, would be up. The Australian's dream fell to the thick pile carpet.

Williamson tried to register a protest or two. He couldn't talk about the anguish he felt, the sheer misery which was pouring through him; experienced Australian jockeys tend not to do that. Nor could he say, as a professional, that Galbreath's promise to pay him an extra riding present – about £6,000 – if Piggott won didn't mean a thing. It was not a time to make the point that even in the world of racing, where money is dominant, there are some things against which you cannot put a price. All Williamson could say which would have any influence on John Galbreath was that he was perfectly fit, but Galbreath was unmoved. He was used to dealing with professional athletes arguing cases in which they had a strong vested interest. Galbreath raised a hand and said, 'If you had been able to ride this day to give everyone, including yourself, proof of your fitness, it would be different. But under the circumstances it would not be fair to anyone. There is no way a jockey who has been out of the saddle for ten days can be at his best.'

We can only speculate on Williamson's feeling of desolation as he walked out of Claridge's. He had so little time left, and John Galbreath had slammed the door on his last chance of winning the big one.

Vincent O'Brien was clearly embarrassed. He was caught between the two jockeys, and of course he had his own instincts. He always kept these close, but it is reasonable to presume that he was anxious for Roberto to be ridden with maximum effect. He had trained Roberto to the point of Derby favouritism. He had built himself a superb reputation as a trainer of classic horses and Roberto had an excellent chance of enhancing the record. Though he had a deep respect for Williamson's skill, it was also true that Piggott had become a vital arm of his spreading empire. It was O'Brien who had first lured Piggott away from Murless, and it was through his hands that the glory of Sir Ivor and Nijinsky had passed. O'Brien found himself deferring to the weight of Galbreath's argument, which was brusque and could be summarized easily enough: 'We have the Derby favourite. Our jockey hasn't ridden for ten days. The best jockey in the world is a phone-call away from leaping on to our horse.'

The decision was practical. On the eve of the race O'Brien declared, 'I just couldn't feel more for Bill Williamson, but when I listened to Mr Galbreath's arguments I was convinced he was right.' Williamson did not lash out. He was totally professional. If Piggott won, Williamson would benefit by £6,000. It would be a cushion against the pain, the feeling of exclusion. He said, cryptically, 'I think Roberto is the form horse. I think he will win.'

One man who couldn't win, at least in the eyes of the public which had hungrily gobbled up the news, was Lester Piggott. If he won, well, he was on the favourite. If he lost there would be the whistle of derision. He would stand convicted of overweening greed. The public was convinced that Piggott, displaying the full weight of his ruthless nature, had touted for the ride, exploited Williamson's embarrassment after the fall at Kempton Park. Like the Australian, Piggott refused to be drawn into a public statement on the issue but, under pressure on the morning of the race, he said with some force: 'I would like to stress that the owner's decision is nothing to do with me. I'm very sorry it happened in this way.' If the public was appalled at what it considered a callous disregard for a man's feelings, it managed to thrust aside its disgust on the way to the bookmaker's office. The public might not be keen on Piggott's ethics, but it had every respect for his riding. Millions poured on Roberto once the switch of jockeys had been announced.

There was open hostility to Piggott at Epsom. The crowd seethed and rumbled as Piggott talked with Galbreath and O'Brien in the paddock. It was as though they were conspirators, partners in some unspeakable crime. It was a fitful day. The sky was a patchwork of blue and white through which a weak sun aimed an occasional ray. Of course, Piggott's face showed no emotion. He was not interested in lip-reading jeers, no more than he was in idle flattery. He had another big job to do.

It was not an impressive Derby field. The betting suggested that the chief threats to Roberto would come from Lyphard, an American-bred contender trained in France and ridden by Freddy Head, and Yaroslav. There was good blood in Yaroslav. His half-sister, Altesse Royale, had had a brilliant 1971, sweeping to victory in the One Thousand Guineas and the Oaks. Though Yaroslav had not raced previously in 1972, his trainer Noel Murless had produced some magical runners from his top hat before and there were rumours of blistering gallops back in Newmarket. At 22–1 there was a colt called Rheingold. Henry Zeisel, who ran a night club in London and in his youth had been lead violinist for the Vienna Philharmonic Orchestra, had sold four-fifths of the colt the day before the race. Partnered by Ernie Johnson, Rheingold was not considered too dangerous, but Piggott respected him. The boos for Piggott were an odd intrusion into the Derby rituals, but inevitable; an English sports crowd has a somewhat excessive regard for the underdog. Anyone who has spent more than an hour at Wimbledon knows that logic, a cool appreciation of the facts, always runs a poor second to emotion.

Piggott took Roberto quietly up to the start. He speculated on how Roberto would show. His mind flickered back down the years.... Never Say Die, Crepello, St Paddy, Sir Ivor, and Nijinsky. It was a wonderful run and now he was a few minutes away from equalling Jem Robinson's century-old record of Derby wins. The great Fred Archer hadn't got this far. It wasn't bad at all. He could stand a few boos.

By Tattenham Corner it was clear that Piggott had nothing to fear from Freddy Head and Geoff Lewis, who were aboard the second favourites. Head, whose ability to navigate English courses is still considered less than phenomenal by most leading English jockeys, went disastrously wide, prompting Roger Mortimer to observe dryly, 'Head, who rides so short he looks to be standing on the horse's withers, was unable to control Lyphard, who went so wide that he appeared desirous of visiting relatives in Putney.' Yaroslav, Lewis later complained, 'spent most of the time looking around. He was never going to do anything. You could say he needed the race.'

Pentland Firth, ridden by Pat Eddery, one of the fast emerging jockeys of a new generation, took it up after two furlongs and he still held the lead coming out of Tattenham Corner. Pentland Firth was pursued by a bunch comprising Meadow Mint, Ormindo, Manitoulin, Palladium, and Mercia Boy, but it did not seem that any great menace lurked in this grouping. More persuasive was the rhythm of Roberto – and Rheingold. Piggott, yet again, had got to Tattenham Corner in perfect shape and now, up that great wide, roaring tunnel was Robinson's record. He could ride through any amount of hostility for that. But he had to make a quick decision. He had planned to ride his classic style, delaying the big move to the last possible moment.

This was because there were still considerable doubts

about Roberto's staying capacity. The problem was that Pentland Firth, clearly tiring, was beginning to lean away from the rails. Rheingold, though running strongly, was drifting towards the rails. Piggott might be denied space in the middle. The gap between Rheingold and Pentland Firth was closing with every stride. So Piggott had to move. It is almost imperceptible, this shifting of weight, this calling to action, when made by a great jockey. Piggott once told Kenneth Harris about the matter of riding a strong finish:

> A lot depends on the horse's balance. If he loses balance, he loses speed and direction, and that might cost him the race – he'll lose, or just get passed the last fifty yards. Part of a jockey's job is to get his horse running balanced and keep him balanced, and this means you have got to be balanced yourself all the time to fit in with the horse. The jockey has his own centre of gravity but he can shift his and the horse can't. At every stride, the horse's centre of gravity is shifting in relation to the jockey's. Getting a horse balanced means keeping your balance, every stride, every second to suit his.

It was clear, even to the most jaundiced eye, that Piggott and Roberto knew all about each other's centre of gravity. Roberto moved grimly through the shrinking gap and though Pentland Firth was to take a bump Piggott had long passed the point when he would carelessly court action from the stewards. Eddery said emphatically, 'The bump only affected me by a length, and it happened because Rheingold bore in on Roberto, it was not Lester's fault.'

They were two hundred yards from the post now, and it was a straight issue between Piggott and Johnson. It was the situation the old fighter John Galbreath had envisaged when he waited, in his suite in Claridge's, for the arrival of Bill Williamson. Everything that happened in the next few blazing seconds, justified Galbreath in his cold decision. Yes, these were definitive moments in the life and the career of Lester Piggott. You might wonder about the finishes on Carrozza and Petite Etoile, the extraordinary release of Sir Ivor's killing bursts, the handling of Nijinsky, but you have to concede that never before had the peculiar driving forces come together so dramatically. The urge to win, whatever the cost in personal popularity, was all there as he and Roberto pounded into the teeth of a hostile crowd and Derby history. Piggott's whip blurred, but he sat quite still.

In a tight finish a strong jockey may seem to be doing nothing in the saddle except throwing his hands forward. That is all you will see but the horse is going flat out, and still going straight. In the same finish, a weaker jockey will be throwing himself about in the saddle, and his horse will be rolling about off balance. Keeping the horse balanced in the last hundred yards, and making him put it all in can take a lot out of a jockey. It's got to be there to start with.

Ernie Johnson, a fine, experienced jockey who had won the Derby on Blakeney in 1969, was simply no match for Piggott over the last hundred yards of the 1972 Derby. Piggott rode with sensational strength and drive. He got Roberto home by a nose. Johnson said afterwards: 'On a flat course, Rheingold would definitely have won, but he was hanging with the camber and giving me no chance to ride him properly.'

There was a hush over Epsom after the announcement that the photo finish decision was for Piggott by a nose, and then another ripple of boos as he brought Roberto into the unsaddling enclosure. In the long wait for the decision, Galbreath, masking his concern that his great ordeal might end with fractional defeat, defended the Piggott decision. He was amazed, but he still felt he had to explain it. He felt a cold wall of censure.

I have had a lot of experience of athletes. My baseball team has just won the World Series. I know something about fitness and I'm convinced that no sportsman who has been out of action for ten days, as Williamson was, can be a hundred per cent. It was that factor and nothing else that brought about the decision.

O'Brien stood by Galbreath's side. He said only, 'Lester gave Roberto a beautiful ride.' He knew that, in the end, his latest Derby triumph owed everyting to Lester Piggott. The professional gambler John Banks was emphatic. He had cheered home Piggott for reasons not entirely based on an objective study of jockeyship and he summed up the situation succinctly enough:

> There has been so much rubbish talked about what has happened over this ride. You saw that today in that last furlong. Old Bill is a great jockey, but he could never have done that job. There's no one in the world who could – except Lester.

The great milling crowd, still gorging itself on its sense of fair play, remained unconvinced. The boos lingered on – and prompted Lord John Oaksey, a distinguished racing writer and brave steeplechase jockey, to comment that of all the men in the world Lester Piggott was probably the least susceptible to the judgements of the crowd. They cheered madly when Williamson, who said, 'I congratulate Piggott' brought in two winners against Piggott, riding two favourites. They didn't it seemed, distinguish between these races and the scale of Piggott's achievement along the last two hundred yards of the Derby. It was a failure of perception which some might say rather confirmed Piggott's aloof attitude. He had expressed sympathy for Williamson and now his mind was on other things. Specifically, Rheingold.

He had been deeply impressed with the big brown colt and shared the general opinion that had he not been on the back of Roberto, Rheingold would have come home the winner. Rheingold could do him a favour some day.

17 Just Doing a Job

On 7 October 1973 at Longchamp, the wonderful racecourse which glows amid the trees, bathed in the soft light of Paris, Piggott would win the last prize to elude his iron grip. He would win the Prix de l'Arc de Triomphe on the back of Rheingold. He would consign to history the failures on Part Top and Nijinsky.

Before then, however, there would be one of those rare moments of fallibility; the reassurance for his rivals that sometimes even Lester Piggott is left with a generous amount of egg on his face. It came just two months after the strained glory of the Roberto ride. Piggott had switched to Rheingold for the Benson and Hedges Gold Cup at York, the American ace Baeza partnering Roberto. It seemed an academic exercise. The great Brigadier Gerard was 3–1 on. He had won fifteen races in succession. Rheingold, whose stock had improved dramatically with the defeat of Hard to Beat in the Grand Prix de Saint Cloud, was at 7–2, and Roberto, who had run listlessly in the Irish Derby, was a derisive 12–1. Roberto's reaction was indignation. Six furlongs out, he roared for the post. The Brigadier gave chase, but such was Roberto's momentum he still had three lengths in hand at the post. Gold Rod in third place was another ten lengths away. Piggott was nowhere and less than happy.

Of course, Rheingold proved a marvellous investment. Piggott drew his dividend in Paris a year later. Earlier in 1973 there had been another 'jocking off' incident when Henry Zeisel and his partners decided to replace Yves St Martin with Piggott. Although there is a great affinity and mutual respect between Piggott and St Martin, a regular house guest at Newmarket, it is fair to say that the mood was not that of blood brothers when they mounted in the Longchamp paddock. St Martin was on Allez France, daughter of the superb Sea Bird II.

Piggott had much to prove at Longchamp. The defeats on Park Top and Nijinsky had run deeply. They were flaws in a masterpiece of a career. His apologists could argue that there were factors working against him on both days, but he had to do something about it, out on the course where it had happened. It was the same kind of business as at Laurel Park, Washington DC a few years earlier.

He left nothing to chance. He was quickly away and was never out of the leading group. Coming into the straight from the long bend, he began to work. He pushed Rheingold alongside Authi and Direct Flight. In the straight Rheingold and Piggott flew. The big bay and the Long Fella stretched out beautifully. St Martin, vigilant but caught, squeezed Allez France along the rails but the swell of sound was to no avail. Piggott and Rheingold had it by two and half lengths. Henry Zeisel was so moved he wanted to reach out for a violin. Piggott settled for the money, and the knowledge that the last great prize had fallen to him.

It was good quality champagne but for Robert Sangster and Vincent O'Brien it might have been vinegar. The problem was the wreckage of the Sangster–O'Brien assault on the 1977 classic season. Sangster, heir to the Vernons pools fortune, had made an alliance with the Irishman which surpassed ambition anything that had happened before in racing. Sangster had set up a world-wide bloodstock and racing empire. He had dallied with racing for many years and started the grandiose operation four years before.

I had reached a point when I knew I could go only two ways. I could put it all on a business footing, make a profit out of pleasure, or I had to pull out. I decided that racing was so important to me that I couldn't think of any other area that was so absorbing, that I had to go into it in a big way. I had met this very impressive chap John Magnier, who was only twenty-four, who had a place in Cork. We pooled our stud operation. My situation in Cheshire was that whenever something came on the market I was the tail-end Charlie in a queue of six.

So I needed to make a massive investment and I had to sell the idea of this self-contained operation to bankers who thought I was mad to talk about putting money into horses. Things happen to horses. But I managed to convince them. I mentioned a few names. Names like Vincent O'Brien and Lester Piggott. Then I had to convince myself. I knew if Vincent O'Brien would come in it was all right. He did and I can't really describe the confidence that gave me. And if I had O'Brien, well, the odds were that I would also have Lester Piggott.

The theory was magnificent. It was a licence to sweep up the great trophies of world racing, but there was no euphoria as the three men sipped their champagne in the spring of 1977. They were sitting in the weighing-room at The Curragh. Sangster and O'Brien had been summoned there by Piggott. It was just three weeks to Derby Day at Epsom and Piggott had some decisions to make. He had badly wanted to ride the Aga Khan's Blushing Groom, a warm favourite, but his overtures had been rejected – firmly. Henry Samani would ride Blushing Groom. The Sangster–O'Brien contender, The Minstrel, had been an appalling disappointment both at Newmarket and The Curragh. Sangster describes the occasion:

I suppose this was a time when I felt most nerves, most apprehension. The winter had been filled with such hopes, such high expectations. We had Cloonara favourite for the Thousand Guineas and The Minstrel for the Two Thousand Guineas. Both were slotted [well beaten]. The Minstrel was beaten again in the Irish Guineas and I was leaving the course with Vincent when we got the message that Lester wanted to see us in the weighing room.

He was sitting there in his vest. His mind was on the Derby. He said that despite the results so far The Minstrel was the best horse at Ballydoyle. Vincent said: 'I'll want to see how the horses are in three or four days time ... if things are okay, well ...' And then I said, 'Lester, if we get a firm commitment that you will ride the horse it's on.' He gave it there and then and I suppose that was a sort of turning point. Minstrel won the Derby – and we showed that we could deliver a big winner.

What Piggott proved, beyond the long-established fact that no one could begin to match his ability to muster power in the last strides to the finish, was that he was utterly crucial to the plans of a man like Robert Sangster. His riding skill had been known for so long. Now he was helping to make decisions involving millions of pounds. Earlier Piggott had been forced into the personal decision of choosing between Hot Grove and The Minstrel for the 1977 Derby. The delicate choice was dramatically confirmed in the last furlong as, inch by inch, The Minstrel wore down Willie Carson's mount. Afterwards Carson said: 'Half a furlong out I thought we would just hang on. Before the race we reckoned there were only three horses who would genuinely get the trip but we found another one and, surprise, surprise, Lester Piggott was on his back.' Blushing Groom was among the non-stayers, finishing five lengths behind The Minstrel and Hot Grove. Later that summer Piggott was to say: 'The Minstrel gave me one of the most exciting Derby rides and he was probably one of the gamest horses of the whole lot. That day Hot Grove had him stone cold a furlong and a half out and from there there was no way he was going to win. But he really tried right to the end and he got there on guts.' Paddy Prendergast, who had so bitterly attacked Piggott at the time of his break with Murless, dwelt more on the sustained brilliance of Piggott's riding. 'Really,' he said, 'that was the finest piece of race riding I have seen. It was just unbelievable the way Piggott stole that race. Really he shouldn't have had a chance. You just have to hold your hands up and say "fantastic".' But if Piggott had reached out for every inch of power and skill in his possession, it was the judgement and the imagination which most impressed Vincent O'Brien. In the after-race throng Vincent O'Brien's soft voice was telling the whole of The Minstrel story. 'Lester believed in him,' said O'Brien. 'He talked me into bringing him to Epsom. We had some doubts – some very serious doubts – but when a man like Lester Piggott speaks you had better listen. I admire him so much as a rider and as a man. His judgement is just marvellous.'

The scale of Piggott's judgement, the implications of his

talk with O'Brien and Sangster in The Curragh weighing room, was established when The Minstrel, bred by Eddie Taylor in Canada, was eventually syndicated for nine million dollars.

Another Sangster–O'Brien horse was Alleged. In 1977 and 1978 Piggott rode Alleged beautifully to successive Arc de Triomphe victories. In 1977 Piggott won from the front. In 1978 he slipped smoothly away from Willie Shoemaker on Trillion. There had been serious doubts about Alleged's second challenge for the world's richest horse-race. Robert Sangster had gone into racing on a vast scale only after making sure of the co-operation of Vincent O'Brien and Lester Piggott, and the autumn of 1978 had been a glorious confirmation of his instincts.

Alleged's second victory was at heart a stunning piece of training – and a marvellous piece of riding. I saw Alleged break the track record over one and a quarter miles three weeks earlier. It hadn't run for four months, but it shattered that record – without breaking out of a hack canter. The only worry I had as we all flew over to Paris was that Alleged had been a little sweaty under the saddle before the run at Longchamp. But Lester said, 'That was only natural. The horse had been off the course for four months.' I said to Lester, 'You have taken away my last doubt.' After the race the French went mad. I spent much time trying to protect Alleged from the hordes. Some people were pulling hairs out of its tail for souvenirs. I looked at this $16 million horse and it wasn't batting an eyelid. I felt this tremendous surge of pride. Pride in the horse and pride that I was working with men like Vincent O'Brien and Lester Piggott. Together their knowledge was, really, breathtaking.

The story of Lester Piggott has so many superb moments: at Epsom in the company of any colt or filly from Never Say Die and Carozza to The Minstrel; at Laurel Park, Washington, in 1969 when he proved to America that which Europe had long absorbed; in Copenhagen when he brought in Pollerton in the Scandanavian Open and those who saw it said they had never seen better, more powerful riding.

In Deauville in August 1979 the French crowd rubbed their eyes and hooted when they realized that Piggott had, indeed, snatched a whip from the hand of French jockey Alain Lequeux. A French radio commentator reported: 'Lequeux had his own whip raised and was just bringing it down when Piggott caught the whip and took it from his hand. He then started using it on his own horse – and came second.' The Deauville stewards banned Piggott for twenty days. His old friend and rival Geoff Lewis said:

> The stewards should have sent him to the Bahamas for a free holiday – the skill involved in that was incredible! I went up to Lester and said 'Good God, what were you thinking about?' and he said: 'Well, he didn't seem to mind at the time and he'd got no chance.' Then a moment later, and with just a hint of a smile on his face, he did say, 'I must admit it looked bad on the telly.' The man is a freak. There had never been anyone like him – and there never will be again.

Soon Lester Piggott will join the ranks of the trainers and will undoubtedly extend his career over yet another aspect of racing. He has long planned the day, and already has stables organized in Newmarket. I asked him about retirement one afternoon between races.

'The key to it,' he said, 'is when you no longer get any enjoyment from it, when it doesn't matter to you whether you win or lose a race. I haven't reached that stage yet – and I doubt if I ever will. So it means I will retire when I can't do it properly any more.'